IMAGES
of America

ANDALUSIA

Located in the heart of Andalusia, this monument to the town's textile industry introduces visitors to the significant impact of textiles on both the town and nation. The tribute inspires reflection on locals' working past and aspirations for an industrious future. Starting with around 25 employees who produced about 125 garments (underwear) per week, Alabama Textile Industry (Alatex) grew from a one-plant, one-product operation to become a textile giant. In 1959, the *Andalusia Star-News* reported that Andala and Alatex had more than 2,400 employees and seven plants turning out thousands of different products each week. A typical week's operation included 252,000 garments, including 120,000 dress shirts and 36,000 sport shirts. This monument weighs 2,500 pounds and stands in nine feet of concrete. It is 13 feet tall and 11 feet wide from elbow to elbow, and the necktie can be changed seasonally. Local draftsman William Merrill built the shirt based on a scale model designed by local artist Larry Strickland. (Photograph by Charles W. White Jr.)

ON THE COVER: This photograph from 1924 shows the industrial sewing room of the Andala textile industry. One had only to tour this plant and the seven other plants built during expansion to appreciate the level of skill and speed these employees exercised. A huge workforce of women kept the machines humming during World War II, as shown in this panoramic image. (Courtesy of Henry Kinsey.)

IMAGES
of America

ANDALUSIA

Kristy Shuford White

ARCADIA
PUBLISHING

Published by Arcadia Publishing
Charleston, South Carolina

Library of Congress Control Number: 2014931060

For all general information, please contact Arcadia Publishing:
Telephone 843-853-2070
Fax 843-853-0044
E-mail sales@arcadiapublishing.com
For customer service and orders:
Toll-Free 1-888-313-2665

Visit us on the Internet at www.arcadiapublishing.com

*To my husband, Charles W. White Jr.; the memory
of my daddy, Franklin L. Shuford Sr.; and my mom,
Janet Salter Shuford, and her AHS class of 1972*

CONTENTS

ACKNOWLEDGMENTS

I have to thank all of my family because inevitably my projects become *their* projects. I would also like to thank the Covington Historical Society and the Three Notch Museum and wish to express gratitude to all who have assisted in the preparation and completion of this book. Sue Bass Wilson, Jan White, and David Walters, who guided me through artifacts at the museum and made the research process a pleasure instead of a burden, were constant in their enthusiasm and support. This work would not be possible without the forethought and perseverance of Henry Kinsey, who has digitized so much of our heritage. To Robert Evers and Denille Spears, who lovingly photographed our historic structures under an intense deadline, I owe a debt of gratitude. I extend thanks to Michele Gerlach and the *Andalusia Star-News*, the *Opp News*, and the following authors for their reference works: Wyley Donald Ward for *Original Land Sales and Grants in Covington County Alabama* and *Early History of Covington County Alabama: 1821–1871*; Gus J. and Ruby R. Bryan for *Covington County History: 1821–1976*, published by the Opp Historical Society; George Sidney Waits Jr. for *E.L. More's River Falls Power Company* and *From the Halls of Montezuma: Sketches of Early Covington County and Andalusia, Alabama History*, and his work with Polly W. Waits for *Newsletters Along the Three Notch Trail*; Sue Bass Wilson for *Historical Riding Tour through Andalusia, Alabama* and her work with Paula Sue Duebelt on *A History of Andalusia, Alabama*; and Solon Dixon as told to John Burgess for *The Dixon Legend*. I have also consulted the compilation *The Heritage of Covington County, Alabama*. I appreciate the staff of the Andalusia Public Library and the Lurleen B. Wallace Community College Library for their assistance in my research. Additionally, the history of local homes provided by retired physician William C. Hansford, Ellie Sentell Etheridge, and the work of Linda Brogden Palmer of the J.W. Shreve Addition Historic District Planning Committee was invaluable. Finally, I offer special thanks to Chuck White, Amber Watson, Jessica Byrd, Destiny Hamid, Greg White, David Wyatt, Jerry Wishum, Steve and Harriet Hubbard, Jared Boutwell, Sandra Burkhardt, Gerry Richards, and Arcadia acquisitions editor Liz Gurley.

I hope you enjoy this photographic glimpse back into Andalusia's history prior to 1950. You can discover what makes this a great' place to live. You may possess a photograph that would have made this book whole, or your photograph could have shed light where I left darkness. I encourage you to contact the Covington Historical Society or the Three Notch Museum and let them scan your artifact and record your story,.so future publications can be complete. All of the author's proceeds from the sale of this book will benefit the Three Notch Museum. The mailing address for the museum is c/o Covington Historical Society, Inc., P.O. Box 1582, Andalusia, AL 36420. Thank you for your support.

Unless otherwise noted in the text, images in this book are provided courtesy of Henry Kinsey and the Three Notch Museum.

INTRODUCTION

Turpentine, timber, trains, and textiles are sure to be synonymous with stories of Andalusia, the county seat of Covington County.

By the summer of 1824, the log courthouse for Covington County had been completed on the eastern side of the Conecuh River. Montezuma had been an attractive location because the Conecuh River could be navigated south to the Pensacola area. Many settlers rafted timber and cotton down the river. A fairly large village developed around the courthouse, but it was not long before Montezuma settlers realized that river living came with its inherent problems in the form of malaria, yellow fever, and flooding. Early settler John Devereaux, who passed through Georgia as he migrated to Alabama, became the first postmaster at Montezuma in 1826 and received a lifelong appointment as a county court judge. His service and contributions are well documented, and the name of the hill where he resided was Devereaux, or Debro Hill, as we know it today. As the county's first state senator and sponsor of the enabling acts that created the county, he is considered the "Father of Covington County."

The town of Andalusia was established on January 16, 1844, when a legislative act was signed naming it as the permanent seat of Covington County. The post office was officially established on July 18, 1844, after the little village of Montezuma had slowly been relocated to the highest point up the hill between the Conecuh and Yellow Rivers, a place of safety on the watershed. By 1850, the population had grown to 50 persons.

Replacing the log courthouse at Montezuma, a two-story square wooden structure was built in the center of town between 1844 and 1845. A jail was also constructed about this time. This first Andalusia courthouse was consumed by fire on January 13, 1878, destroying all the records. The second courthouse in Andalusia was a two-story frame one with four limestone chimneys, two on each side. It was destroyed by fire in October 1895. The third courthouse was the two-story brick one with a clock tower built in the center of town square in 1897 that served the county for about 20 years. In 1916, the present courthouse, a much larger facility, was built. The granite and marble landmark building designed by architect Frank Lockwood is probably the fourth courthouse in Andalusia.

The first buildings around the square were wooden, and businesses, livery stables, boardwalks, balconies, and saloons lined the grid of dirt streets. Patrons of the saloon could buy their refreshments in clay jugs and return the jugs to be refilled.

Progress slowed throughout the South when the War Between the States ravaged the nation. Alabama joined the Confederacy and seceded from the Union in 1861. Men and boys left to join and fight for the cause, while women and children strived to keep the farms going. By 1868, Alabama rejoined the union. Andalusia officially incorporated as a town in 1888. By 1897, the town boasted nine new businesses, several boardinghouses, and a newly completed brick courthouse located in the center of the square. The nationally recognized Horse Shoe Lumber Company was organized in answer to the growing demand for lumber and railroad ties.

Nearly 60 years elapsed between the time the first railroad was planned and when the first track was built in the county. As railroad companies contemplated possible Southern routes, James Austin Prestwood organized locals eager to extend the railroad line into Andalusia from Searight. In 1898, the following businessmen moved to Andalusia from Searight and became instrumental in town development: Jim Rainer, John Simms, Lake Gantt, Athan Boyette, Ben Perrett, William Shreve, William Knox, Tom Brown, Ike Roseberg, Walter Lowman, Abe Sachs, Dr. Ed Broughton, and Tom Clarke. The Central of Georgia Railway finally completed the Searight extension in September 1899, and by the next year the population of Andalusia had nearly doubled to 500.

The trains left Andalusia carrying agricultural and timber products. They returned with building materials for constructing new houses springing up on the main streets, seafood from

New Orleans, mules for hauling, and travelers passing through. With the availability of building materials, many families built beautiful homes lining East Three Notch, South Three Notch, River Falls, and Church Streets. Families continued to migrate from Florida and Georgia, including the Alphonso Beauregard Council Darling family and the Georgia Orkney Waits family, whose stately homes still proudly stand on East Three Notch Street.

The 1920s roared in, and the population was pushing 2,500. E.L. More and C.A. O'Neal, partners in the Horse Shoe Lumber Company, constructed the hydroelectric dams and generating facilities at Point "A" and Gantt to bring permanent power to the area. Prior to this, a much smaller generating facility downtown at the Central Street power plant produced minimal electricity.

About this time, a German immigrant named John George Scherf arrived on the scene as secretary of the Andalusia Chamber of Commerce. Fluent in seven languages and with an international background in textiles, he was a visionary who helped shape Andalusia's economy. After four years with the chamber, he resigned in 1923 to become organizer and manager of the Andala Company. This textile business lasted over 70 years with branches in South Alabama and Northwest Florida. J.G. Scherf was elected mayor in 1932 and served in this office for 16 years—the longest term of any mayor. In 1935, he built his home on East Three Notch Street. Springdale, as it was called, is still one of the most impressive historic homes in the old Andalusia residential district and is now owned by the City of Andalusia.

The 1920s ended with a bust. By 1929, banks crashed and the Great Depression consumed the nation. In the midst of the national crisis, the Andalusia area faced a local catastrophe with the flood of 1929 when both dams on the Conecuh were breached.

The 1930s were harsh, but progress still continued. The Commercial Bank opened its doors in 1933, and in 1934 a group of leading businessmen met to organize a federal savings and loan association to promote home ownership.

In 1935, a butane gas plant was built and streetlights as well as fire hydrants were installed around the square. The public library found a home on the corner of College Street and Sixth Avenue in 1936. Because lumber was still a plentiful and valuable resource, the Dixon Lumber Company was founded in 1939 by Charles, Jess, and Solon Dixon. The Dixons, national pioneers in forest management, are known for their view of the forest as a renewable resource.

Around 1940, a group of 14 Rural Electric Administration (REA) co-ops in Alabama and Northwest Florida formed the Alabama Electric Cooperative to generate and transmit wholesale electric power and expand the availability of electrical power to rural areas. Today, PowerSouth meets the energy needs of nearly a million consumers. Locally, Covington Electric Cooperative and the City of Andalusia, both members of PowerSouth, serve the energy needs of over 28,000 members. New and improved sewer and natural gas utilities were provided. The textile industry expanded, and the Covington County Bank opened its doors in 1947. The South Alabama Gas District was incorporated in 1952.

The worldwide flu epidemic resulted in Andalusia's hospital care beginning as Covington County Hospital in 1918. This first hospital was a converted Victorian house on the corner of Watson and South Three Notch Streets, with Dr. T.Q. Ray as the chief of staff. A modern brick facility known first as Andalusia City Hospital and later as Covington Memorial on East Watson Street followed. In 1943, a second hospital facility was opened by Dr. Ray Evers on Hillcrest Drive. It was incorporated in 1947 as Hillcrest Infirmary. The hospital began with 43 beds. By 1985, this hospital had changed from Columbia General to Columbia Regional and boasted the only female hospital CEO in the state of Alabama, Sybil Barton. After nearly 50 years, this facility closed. Current medical needs are served by Andalusia Regional Hospital, a 100-bed, acute care accredited medical-surgical facility located on South Three Notch Street.

Today, Andalusia's largest employer is Shaw Industries (formerly Amoco Fabrics and Fiber Company), a carpet yarn manufacturing plant. Andalusia is Shaw's largest facility and the world's largest polypropylene BCF operation. It is also home to the world's largest Volmann twister carpet yarn installation.

One

GOVERNMENT

Leolive Benson (left) and Mildred Gantt are pictured in front of the 1895 courthouse in their horse and buggy. The courthouse, the third in Covington County's short history, touted a clock and a bell. Residents and merchants depended on seeing the clock from a distance or hearing the bell toll to move about their daily routine. The courthouse stood in the middle of the public square and faced east. The bricks used in construction were made on-site, according to early records. Other materials were hauled from Searight, then the rail terminus.

In 1821, more than 6,000 acres of land around Montezuma was purchased, most of it for $1.25 per acre. At Montezuma, there was a courthouse (Covington County's first), saloon, hotel, livery stable, racetrack, docking facilities, and warehouses. This photograph of Montezuma was taken in 1901, long after the small community was moved to higher land.

Covington County's frame courthouse was destroyed by fire in 1895. (The first courthouse had also been consumed by fire in 1878.) It was a beautiful white-painted structure, and on the ground floor a wide hall ran through the building both ways, cutting that floor up into four offices, one in each corner. The roof had no gables. The house in the background belonged to Becky Smith. She was a Dixon before she married.

The first brick courthouse was built in the middle of the court square. The contract for this building was signed in December 1895. The contractor was B.C. Williams of Hazlehurst, Georgia, and the architect was W. Chamberlin & Company of Knoxville, Tennessee. Judge Malachi Riley was judge of probate at the time of the contract. Work on the building was begun on August 1, 1896, and finished on April 1, 1897. The building had seven rooms on the first floor and four rooms on the second. Its courtroom proper was the largest and most convenient courtroom in the 12th Judicial Circuit. It was conceded to be, by far, the best courthouse south of Montgomery.

This is the Masonic service for laying the cornerstone of the Covington Courthouse seen in the previous image, which was completed in 1897. The steeple had a four-face clock, generally classified during those days as the "poor man's pocket watch." Four-faced tower clocks were sometimes the only way to tell time in a community. The clock could be seen from some distance away in all directions. The striking of the clock could be heard for a mile. This courthouse only stood 21 years before it was torn down in 1918. The bell was saved and is now placed in the front lawn of the present courthouse.

As the city of Andalusia and Covington County grew, long-term planning began to determine infrastructure needs, like paving. A debate waged on whether the current courthouse should live out its usefulness or whether a new one should be built before a paving project was implemented. The new courthouse won out and was constructed in 1916 at a cost of $135,000. The c. 1912 jail is visible behind it.

This view of the public square reveals (to the left of the square) P. Lewis Jewelers, Brown and Broughton Druggists, and the c. 1921 First National Bank building; (in the center) Kilpatrick and Mashburn Furniture and Hardware, the Bank of Andalusia, and S.D. Brooks; and (to the right) Tisdale Hardware. Originally, a Confederate monument was planned for the circle in the middle of the park square. The plaza was maintained by the garden clubs and is remembered by previous generations for its chinaberry trees.

Attorney Ed Reid, who was struck with colon cancer in 1942, became the first person in the entire country to read the seven danger signs of cancer on the radio. *Cancer* was a dreaded word, a death sentence to most, and oftentimes doctors would not even tell their patients of the diagnosis. Reid was cured of cancer because of the early detection and prompt treatment. The American Cancer Society presented Reid with an award for his work and devotion to take his story nationwide.

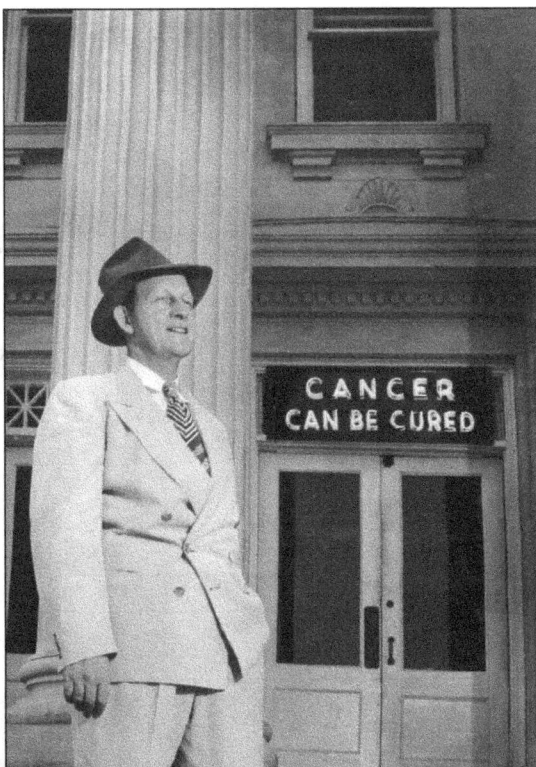

Beautiful architectural details grace the inside of the courtrooms, including this one on the second floor pictured during a public meeting. A stonecutter formed many of the decorative features seen around the majestic building. The interior is centered on an octagonal atrium with floors of white marble and walls of gray marble. (Courtesy of Andalusia Public Library.)

COVINGTON COUNTY COURTHOUSE LATE 30'S

This courthouse, shown here in early 1930s, was built on the north side of the square. Frank Lockwood of Montgomery was the architect, and Little and Clecker Company of Anniston was the builder. The "Old Jail" and the courthouse were listed in the National Register of Historic Places in 1989.

Sen. Lister Hill is speaking in one of the Andalusia courtrooms to residents of Covington County about the dangers of cancer in 1949. Covington County became known as the most cancer-conscious county in the state of Alabama due to the untiring efforts of attorney Ed Reid and the support of the Parnassus Club. (Courtesy of Andalusia Public Library.)

Under the progressive administration of Mayor John G. Scherf, who spent 16 years in office, city finances were stabilized, streets were paved and named, the Clean City Award was received more than once, industry was encouraged, the library grew, schools were labeled among the best, an airport and a new city cemetery were established, and new buildings like this city hall on Opp Avenue were dedicated. Today, the Andalusia Police Department is headquartered here. (Courtesy of the Scherf family and City of Andalusia.)

Mayors of Andalusia included B.H. Lewis (1884–1885), pictured; J.F. Thomas (1885–1888); Ed T. Albritton (1888–1899, first under incorporation); Henry Opp (1899–1906); T.E. Henderson (1906–1908); Z.D. Studstill (1908–1912); J.W. Shreve (1912–1912); A.R. Powell (1912–1914); S.H. Gillis (1914–1918); T.E. Henderson (1918–1924); J. Morgan Prestwood (1924–1927); J.F. Carson (1927–1932); J.G. Scherf (1932–1948); and T.B. Wilder (1948–1956). Note that Andalusia was incorporated twice. (Courtesy of Three Notch Museum.)

On the official Andalusia flag, blue represents the water of the Conecuh River, a source of transportation and trade; white is the color of the courageous and legendary Andalusian horse Destinado, whose remains were buried beneath a tree with the name Andalusia carved into it; and green is symbolic of community growth. The flag's gold trim is a reminder of Andalusia's valuable heritage. The shield and pikes signify Spanish explorers who once came through South Alabama; the horse represents Indian influence; the tree and river are synonymous with the area's journey through history; a plow symbolizes the farmers who settled in the community; the train and pine boughs represent how the railroad and timber industry transformed a village into a bustling town. (Courtesy of Sue Bass Wilson.)

The *Pride of Andalusia*, an L-5 flying ambulance, was piloted by Donald Mock of Andalusia in the Philippine Islands during World War II. Mock, who took this photograph of his crew, was the recipient of the Air Medal with two oak-leaf clusters. He named the aircraft in honor of his hometown.

16

The 31st Alabama "Dixie Division" was photographed in front of the East Three Notch School prior to World War I. Two young men were the first Andalusia casualties, and the VFW Battle-Malcomb Post 3453 was named in their honor. Lee Otis Battle, age 18, was the son of Dr. and Mrs. H.E. Battle of 217 Church Street; he was seaman 2nd class, US Navy, and went missing April 20, 1918, aboard the USS Cyclops. "All hands lost" was the official word by the Navy Department on June 4, 1918. "Only God and the sea know what happened to this ship," stated Pres. Woodrow Wilson. No wreckage was ever found. James Malcomb, age 27, was the son of Mr. and Mrs. Marion A. Malcomb of College Street; he was first lieutenant, Company M, 167 Infantry Rainbow Division, Alabama National Guard, and was killed in action September 13, 1918, in the Argonne Woods, France.

Mary Olive Henderson's mother is shown here holding the American flag during wartime. This image was featured on a local postcard. (Courtesy of the Charles Gantt family.)

The first mail came into the area by way of riders since there were no post offices. The written message was simply delivered personally or given to someone to make the delivery. Previously, the post office was located in rented buildings around town. In this photograph, the first Andalusia Post Office building on South Three Notch Street is under construction. It was built in 1925 at a cost of $50,000.

Reconstruction laws passed in 1866 and 1867 severely hampered the reestablishment of the postal service in the Southern states. The loyalty oath, required by postmasters and mail contractors during the Reconstruction period, was so restrictive concerning the applicant's Confederate activities that it was nearly impossible to find any man in Covington County who was qualified to take the oath. Therefore, for the first time, women began to apply for these positions. Between 1868 and 1872, all the postmasters were women. Here, construction is nearing completion on the new 1925 post office.

18

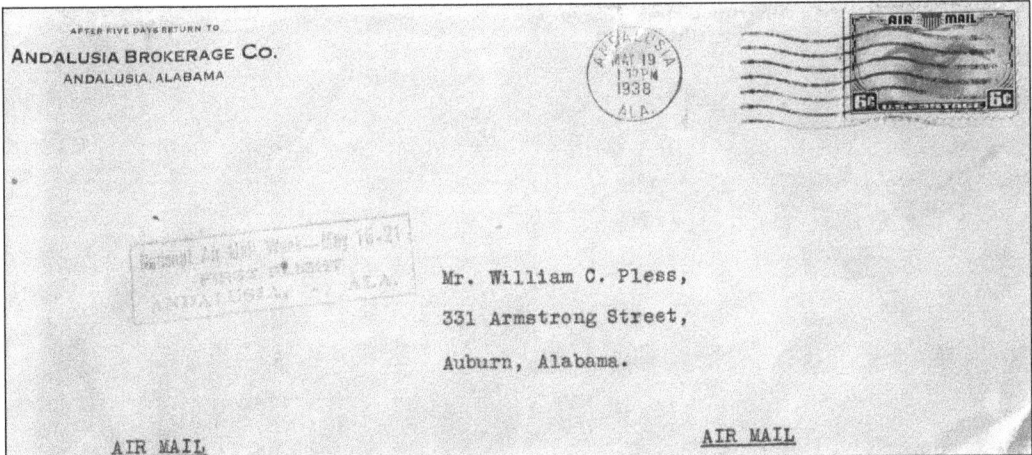

This postal artifact is on display at the Three Notch Museum and commemorates Andalusia's first airmail flight in 1938. Although mail was delivered and probably picked up at the courthouse, there was no post office established in Covington County until 1826, with John W. Devereaux listed as its first postmaster. Charles Dixon built the first Andalusia airport on the old Florala Road in 1929. (Photograph by Charles W. White Jr.)

The first airmail flight in Andalusia was not until May 1938 at the Dixon Airport on Highway 55 South. Standing in front of the airplane are, from left to right, M.H. O'Neal, patrolman Raymond Carlton, postmaster W.B. Wilder, E.L. King, ? Newman, B.B. Padgett, and Stella Beasley.

Andalusia was one of the first post offices in the state to have motorized mail carriers. The motorized service began in October 1915 and replaced horse-and-buggy service. This photograph shows the post office's Ford Model T touring cars. Standing from left to right of the tree are Jim F. Brawner, postmaster; unidentified; and postal clerks Homer Garrett and Lanford Cook. The other three standing are unidentified. In the cars, from left to right, are Clyde Brawner, Barney L. Graves, L. Pearl Driggers, B.B. Padgett, and J.P. Stanley, carriers of the five Andalusia routes. Note the new paved sidewalk but unpaved streets. This was at the old post office on the north side of East Three Notch Street.

Crime did not pay in the late 1920s. Here, moonshine is being destroyed during Prohibition by Sheriff Nat Livings, Deputy Talley, and H.H. Marlin. The men are not specifically identified in this image.

In this photograph, a new fire truck is being presented to the City of Andalusia. The 1940 city council is pictured with Engine No. 2. From left to right are A.C. Wilder Sr. (council), H.H. "Hub" King (council), R.B. "Bob" Albritton (city attorney), W.M. "Bill" Thweatt (council), S.J. (Sanford) McGowin (council), J.G. Scherf (mayor), Hyacinth H. Ellis (city clerk), and L.S. "Luther" Taylor Sr. (council). The fire truck was purchased on June 14, 1940, for $7,885.

Fire destroys the old Paramount Theatre in downtown Andalusia. The fire started Friday afternoon, January 5, 1940. It was believed to have been caused by the heating system. People looked for refuge by gathering on the front steps and entryway of the old First Baptist Church. A large group also gathered by the courthouse. School was dismissed so the children could view the fire.

Covington County's first brick jail was built around 1896. It stood just to the left of center of the site of the courthouse today. One of the first jailers was Jim Padgett, or "Black Smith Jim," as he was known. He and his family lived on the first floor and the prisoners were housed upstairs. A beautiful replacement was built on the same block in 1916, as seen on this historic postcard.

The replacement jail designed by Frederick Ausfield is listed in the National Register of Historic Places. The fortresslike structure gave temporary and permanent residents a view of Magnolia Cemetery. The structure was used primarily from 1916 to 1995. In 1901, the jail was involved in one of Alabama's only cases of martial law, under Sheriff Bradshaw. Local folklore reports paranormal activity at the historic jail. (Courtesy of Sue Bass Wilson.)

Two

RELIGION

The First Baptist Church has kept pace with the growth and development of Andalusia. First known as the Missionary Baptist Church, it joined the association in 1852 (according to old Bethlehem Association minutes) with 25 members. In serving the community's needs, the First Baptist Church has provided four meetinghouses. This structure was finished in 1909 (or 1911, depending upon the record consulted) and cost $50,000. It was located adjacent to the present courthouse. Magnolia Cemetery was established behind it.

The church experienced considerable growth even during Depression years. In March 1926, Dr. Levi Elder Barton became pastor, serving until 1929. Later, a beautiful brick pastorium was erected on a church-owned lot that became part of the grounds for today's First Baptist Church at 700 East Three Notch Street. Pictured here is the framework for the current structure dedicated in 1958. The new sanctuary seats 796 and stands as a beacon on the main street.

Comparing this image with the one on page 23 shows that the church withstood time and watched its neighbors change from a mule-and-wagon business to a progressive theater. The building was cleared of all debt by 1914. It featured beautiful stained-glass windows and a bell tower. According to Muriel Wood Taylor, attempting to ring the First Baptist Church bells at midnight was a popular New Year's Eve escapade among teenagers. Unfortunately, it was razed by the wrecking ball around 1959, stained-glass windows and all, after the new church was built on East Three Notch Street.

Dr. John Jeffers, pastor from 1950 to 1958, and the members of First Baptist decided to relocate the church site about 1955 to a main-street residential area where parking would be abundant. The present church auditorium was dedicated in 1958, and the next year an educational wing and chapel were added, enhancing the beauty of East Three Notch Street. These two building programs were completed at a cost of approximately $600,000. (Courtesy of Sue Bass Wilson.)

The First United Methodist Church began in 1877 when the Reverend W.H. Hasty began to preach in Andalusia. He organized the Methodist Society with 26 charter members. The first building was this white, wooden structure on Church Street. Prior to the days of automobiles, funerals caskets were escorted to Magnolia Cemetery two blocks away by pallbearers on foot. When the congregation built a new church in 1925 on East Three Notch, the Andala Corporation put sewing machines in the building. The structure was subsequently destroyed by fire. (Courtesy of David Walters.)

According to the *Covington News*, on March 2, 1925, the Sunday schools of the First United Methodist Church marched as one body from the old to the new church, marking a great day not only for this denomination but also for the city as a whole. The carillons in the belfry, donated by the Scherf family, played beautiful melodies regularly.

The First United Methodist Church building is an imposing structure—beautiful in design and impressive in appearance, fronting East Three Notch Street. It features one of the finest pipe organs, a product of Austin Organ Company and installed at a cost of $11,200. One of the best choirs that might be found in a smaller city is heard here at all services. The large basement provides space for banquets, social meetings, and gatherings and is equipped for all conveniences, including table service for 100 guests. An administrative and education wing was added in 2000. (Courtesy of Sue Bass Wilson.)

Presbyterians located in Covington County as early as 1825, but it was not until December 5, 1901, that a group of nine assembled in the white frame Methodist church on Church Street (the only church building in Andalusia at that time). The purpose of that meeting was to organize a congregation, which later met in the old courthouse or the First National Bank. Duncan McArtan and Duncan A. McRainey had built the opera house in 1904 over their Andalusia Bank and Trust Company on the corner of Pear and South Three Notch Streets. They donated the land, and ambitious pastor F.G. Hartman took his ability to raise funds with his knowledge of architecture and carpentry and began building the oldest church landmark still standing in Andalusia. It was ready for occupancy in 1908.

Though enlarged and redecorated frequently, the building has changed little in appearance since it was designed by Montgomery architect Carl B. Cooper. Three steeples have risen over the narthex after winds destroyed the first two. Beautiful stained-glass windows, each with symbolic messages, grace all walls. A pipe organ was added in 1926. The building was officially dedicated in 1914, but no offering was taken, since the church had no indebtedness.

The women of the congregation organized in 1907 as the Ladies Aid and Missionary Society; they helped furnish the church through fundraising bazaars, turkey dinners, oyster suppers, and contests. The communion table and baptismal font were added later and were built by Southern Craftsman, a local manufacturer of reproduction Victorian furniture. An education building was added to the First Presbyterian Church PCUSA in 1946.

Although Episcopalians were meeting in Andalusia as early as 1912, it was not until 1948 that St. Mary's Episcopal Church was formally recognized as a mission congregation of the Diocese of Alabama. A church building and parish hall were constructed in 1949 at 205 Second Avenue. Walter Merrill, member of St. Mary's and part owner of Andalusia Manufacturing, and Ed Sturgis, carpenter and finisher, did much of the construction, including producing the altar, lectern, pulpit, baptismal font, and credence table. The church was moved to 1307 East Three Notch Street in 1999. St. Mary's has developed significant ministries to help the hungry and poor in addition to being known for beautiful sacred worship in the historic tradition of the Episcopal Church. (Photograph by Robert Evers.)

Three

EDUCATION

On February 2, 1902, the East Three Notch lot was purchased from Anna Chapman Riley for $1,000, and a brick school building was erected. The contract for Andalusia's first grammar school building was let. W.L. Frazier, of Andalusia, was the lowest, being $7,980, and was therefore awarded the contract. The contract required Frazier to make a bond of $2,500 for the faithful performance of his duty and called for the completion of the building by August 15, 1902. Other builders argued that there was no way the school could be raised for less than $10,000.

The 1902 building served students until about 1912, when a bond issue was organized for the purpose of building a new school to accommodate a growing enrollment of city school students. L.E. Brown, who was made superintendent in 1913, urged that instead of an addition, a completely new and larger building be constructed. His recommendation was accepted. The present East Three Notch Elementary School was constructed in 1914–1915 at a cost of $100,000 for the building and its equipment. The purpose of this building was to house both high school students and those in the lower grades.

This photograph shows the Andalusia High School band in the fall of 1939, under the direction of Sammy Maddox, head majorette (far left) and Mark McGowin (far right). Even though the band members, grades 7–12, attended the present high school on Church Street, this particular image was taken on the front steps of East Three Notch School.

The Andalusia City Schools grew so rapidly that a new high school had to be built. This new building with Mission Revival architecture was constructed by Andalusia Development Company and designed by Frederick Ausfeld and Carl B. Cooper. This building was begun in 1923 with an estimated cost of $50,000, but it was not completed until 1929 with a total cost of $60,000. The basement was not completed until 1935. With continuous student growth, this structure housed the high school until 1940 and then served as an elementary school until 2000.

Pictured in the early 1930s touting their Bulldog spirit are, from left to right, cheerleaders Helen O'Neal, Nell Raborn, and Sara Waits. Athletics have always had a strong tradition at Andalusia High School and a hall of fame has been established to recognize significant contributions. The 1947 undefeated Andalusia Bulldogs football team is one example—inducted for its 10-0 season, during which the Bulldogs scored 290 points and gave up only 13 points.

The present Andalusia High School was completed in 1939 at a total cost of $140,000 and included a 40-acre tract of land on Third Avenue. Tradition runs deep for AHS graduates, who religiously come back to Andalusia each year for the annual homecoming festivities. The Heritage Room is housed in the old main and was established by the class of 1948 under the leadership of Joseph Wingard, English teacher at AHS for 39 years, whose memorabilia collection is significant.

Students met in the Andalusia High School gym for events until an auditorium was constructed in 1964. This 1949 event in the gym was sponsored by the Parnassus Club, which had embarked on a campaign to promote cancer awareness. (Courtesy of Andalusia Public Library.)

Four

HOSPITALITY AND LEISURE

In the early 1900s, the Andalusia's Dixie Hotel was among the most elaborate and most modern hotels in this section of the state. It was owned and operated by B.H. Zeagler and in later years was taken over by J.J. Moates. During the early years, the hotel was patronized by transient guests and traveling salesmen. The hotel was within 30 yards of the L&N Railroad station, and travelers usually arrived on the late-afternoon train.

The Dixie Hotel (pictured here) had competition from other hotels, including the Riley House, City Hotel, and Hotel Ray. The Riley House was located one block west on South Three Notch Street. The Brunson Hotel, also known as City Hotel, was located right next door to the Dixie. Fire ravaged the Dixie Hotel one Thanksgiving morning, and Merrill Motors car dealership was later built on the site.

The City Hotel on South Cotton Street, one block from both railway stations (the Central of Georgia and the L&N), owned and operated by M.E. Brunson, was built and established around 1905 or 1906. Old letterheads advertise "Clean Rooms," "Hot and Cold Water," and "European Plan," which meant that accommodations did not include meals. In this interior photograph of City Cafe, two customers await service from a waitress and M.E. Brunson. In this informal setting, he specialized in short orders such as hamburgers. (Courtesy of Sue Bass Wilson.)

Originally called Hotel Ray, this building was owned and operated by Dr. Ray and located on the south side of Pear Street, between the Opera House and the Thagard Drug Company (Pelham Building). Dr. Gordon L. Wood had an office upstairs in the drugstore. Patients went through the store to go up to Dr. Wood's office—a good business arrangement for Thagard. Later, part of the building was remodeled and became the Victoria Hotel. It was operated by J.J. Moates, who formerly operated the Dixie Hotel before it was destroyed by fire.

William Riley and his wife, Dora, were among the first families to come to Andalusia. William was born in 1840 and Dora in 1844. By 1890, they had children Joel H., Philippa, Fred, Martha, Fannie Bell, and Ida Lee. Railroad officials arriving in Andalusia at the turn of the century often stayed with the Riley family because there were no other overnight accommodations. The Riley home eventually became famous for its comfortable accommodations and good food. This Andalusia hotel became a local landmark on the north side of the L&N Railroad track on South Three Notch Street.

The Gables Hotel was built across from Church Street School by Hyacinth H. "Mom" Ellis, city clerk and treasurer for a number of years. Her daughter Grace Ellis Larson, Andalusia's premier hostess, inherited The Gables from her mother. Many people moving into Andalusia after World War II started out by staying in the adjacent hotel and Gable Apartments. A baby grand piano graced the entrance gathering area for the enjoyment of all.

The Gables Restaurant was the social gathering place for many years and featured smorgasbord lunches, memorable weddings, wedding rehearsal parties, festive dinner parties, anniversary receptions, and bridge parties. Here, the Gables kitchen staff prepares lunch.

36

The local National Guard Armory on Through Street was decorated for a wedding in the early 1930s. It was an elaborate affair with full place settings. During World War II, this building, which was used for county fairs and was previously occupied as Southern Craftsman Furniture, was the site for an internment camp for German prisoners of war. Treated well, these men were hired out to farm families. Many Germans continued to communicate with the Andalusia families after the war ended.

Citizens turned out on East Three Notch Street and the public square in downtown Andalusia to celebrate Armistice Day on November 11, 1918. This scene was photographed from the old courthouse in the center of the public square, just prior to its demolition. This quote from the *Greenville Advocate* on April 29, 1891, memorializing the deceased Confederates, is a fitting tribute that still expresses the sentiments of patriotic Andalusia citizens today: "Time may roll on into eternity, new generations be born, grow up and die, but so long as memory lasts and the spark of love and pride exists in the heart of man, just so long will honor be done to those who fell in battle, just so long will this honor find expression annually in a day set apart in memoriam."

Entertainment can always be found in Andalusia in the form of music or theater. Through the years, local high school productions or community theater programs have provided public performances, like this early production of *The Stockings*. Currently, public performances are produced locally by Act One and the AHS Choral Department, and Covington Arts Council provides the funding for professional touring groups to be brought to Andalusia to perform at the Solon and Martha Dixon Center for the Performing Arts on the campus of Lurleen B. Wallace Community College.

Standing on the sidewalk in front of the First United Methodist Church, members of the Andalusia Shriners salute area Boy Scouts in this early-1930s parade photograph. The Shriners are, from left to right, Bert Windham, C.O. Mathews, John F. Carson, E.O. Baldwin, Clarence Boutwell, two unidentified, Frank Buck, Johnson Carson, H.J. Brogden, and Lester Thagard.

This World War II photograph shows the joint Lions Club and Boy Scouts project to gather aluminum for the war effort. In the foreground at left are one-armed-bandit slot machines that had been confiscated when the late Tom Head was Covington County sheriff. From left to right are (first row, to the right of the sign) Bob Beasley, postmaster H.L. Mullins, Vester Turner, Jess Merrill, Emmette Foreman, and Luther Taylor Jr.; (second row, to the right of the sign) Sheriff Tom Head, Raymond Shreve, John Beasley, H.L. "Red" Campbell, Laurin Avant, Dr. W.R. Middleton, J.H. Johnson, Leland Morris, Guy Cargill, and Abner Powell II; (third row, behind the sign) Boy Scouts Frank Cook, Jimmy Taylor, John Boyette, Wendell Taylor, Harold Avant, Bill Brown, Richard Kearley Jr., Bob Taylor, Dwight McGraw, and unidentified. The Prestwood Building is in the background.

With the mild climate found in Andalusia, spending outdoor afternoons at local rivers or lakes is always a fine way to pass the time. In 1916, these Andalusia friends met at the river for an afternoon picnic. The beach below Prestwood Bridge was also a popular spot for an outing. (Courtesy of the Charles Gantt family.)

Since acquiring Springdale, the City of Andalusia has opened the gates and grounds to area schoolchildren for annual Easter egg hunts. Pictured here are brother and sister Frank and Betty Shuford of Warner Robins, Georgia, visiting Andalusia for Easter. Frank Shuford would later meet his wife in Andalusia and make his family home in Opp, Alabama. He later served on the Covington County Water Board. (Courtesy of the Frank Shuford family.)

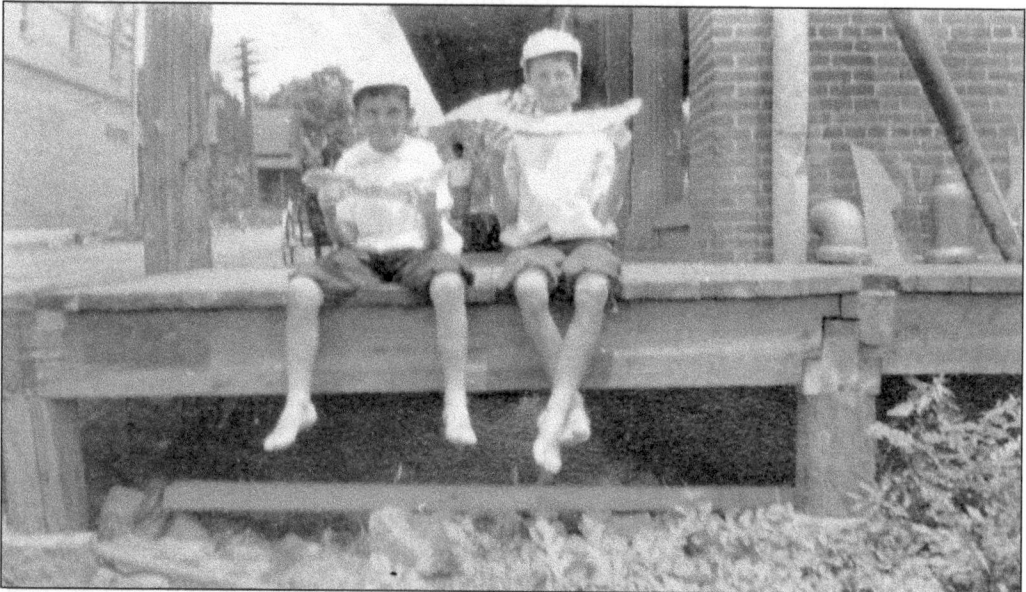

Paul (left) and Leon Zeaglar eat a watermelon on the porch of Benson Hardware in 1916. The watermelon was grown locally, and the porch was a frequent gathering place for adults and children. (Courtesy of the Charles Gantt family.)

Athletics have always been popular and well supported in Andalusia. A 1917 semiprofessional baseball team was sponsored by the Andalusia Packing Plant. Another team, the Andalusia Arrows, perhaps Andalusia's most well-known semipro team, named for a local shirt manufacturing company, was honored in 2010 for its 1938–1962 teams, which included players like Virgil "Fire" Trucks, the former ace pitcher for the Detroit Tigers' Class D team in Andalusia, who played for six Major League teams. He got the nickname "Fire" from an Alabama sportswriter in 1938, when he struck out some 419 batters, according to the *Detroit Times*. (Courtesy of the Charles Gantt family.)

The MacDowell Music Club was organized on April 12, 1919. Here, the club's parade car is driven by Pauline Riley, with Nannie Belle Shaver Waits sitting beside her. Among those in the backseat are Mrs. J.M. Prestwood and Mrs. T.F. Plummer; the others are unidentified. To further celebrate music and the event "Absolutely Andalusia, Homecoming 2010," "Andalusia in Revue" was presented at LBWCC. The performance was a history of Andalusia—from the Indian days to the present—in songs, dances, and skits featuring local talent, with over 200 people participating.

The Andalusia Mentor Club celebrated its yearly social by dressing in the fashion of *Gone with the Wind* at the Avant home on Sanford Road. Carolyn Rankin played the part of the maid, and only her white apron can be seen beside column on the left. From left to right are (first row) Julia Hamner, Inez Riley, Catherine Taylor, Abbie Henderson, Nannie Belle Waits, Mary Fuller, Hazel Shreve, Nan Simmons, Grace Jones, Robbie Lorraine, Mae Reynolds Beall, and Celeste Avant; (second row) Maude Henderson, Catherine Avant, Wilma Woodham, Annelee Dugger, Mrs. Folsom, Ruth Reid, and Mrs. Clifton Coffee. Abbie Henderson arrived to the social in Pony Henderson's buggy. The horses' ears are barely visible over Celeste Avant's shoulder. The Mentor Club was organized on December 30, 1921. Its motto was "Not Failure, but Low Aim is Crime."

The scrapbook pictured, handcrafted by Southern Craftsman Furniture Company, was illustrated by Gladys Mathews Reid and is preserved at the Andalusia Public Library. The Parnassus Club was photographed at the county courthouse in 1949. As part of the federated Women's Clubs, members participated in service projects. This project focused on educating the public about the warning signs of cancer. A "Cancer Can Be Cured" sign is visible in the background. (Courtesy of the Andalusia Public Library.)

Five

HOMES OF DISTINCTION

Perhaps no historic main street home in Andalusia is more significant than Springdale. Built for Alatex president and former mayor J.G. Scherf and his family in the 1930s, it was on the auction block when local physician Dr. Charles Tomberlin retired and decided to downsize. Current mayor Earl Johnson stated, "It is simply impossible to imagine what Andalusia would be today without Mr. Scherf's vision and leadership. I think it is not a stretch to consider John G. Scherf Sr. as the father of modern Andalusia. Of course the great Alatex no longer exists. It is only a memory with Springdale estate being one of the few remaining connections to that historic era." (Photograph by Robert Evers.)

Springdale is composed of approximately four acres, and the beautiful main house is of Mediterranean design with a large four-car garage, a guesthouse, a small pond, several fountains, and beautifully landscaped lawns. It is said that Scherf visited and greatly admired Henry Flagler's home Whitehall (now known as the Henry Morrison Flagler Museum) in Palm Beach, Florida, and returned to Andalusia determined to build a house of similar design. Carl B. Cooper designed the residence. (Courtesy of the Scherf family and the City of Andalusia.)

The back courtyard of Springdale boasts a huge marble table in the center perfect for outdoor receptions or gatherings. Pictured by the courtyard fountain in 1936 are two of Scherf's children, John George Scherf Jr. and Ruth Aurelia Scherf. (Courtesy of the Scherf family and the City of Andalusia.)

When the nation urged citizens to support the war effort by donating all metal products, Mayor J.G. Scherf (second from left) led the effort by removing the iron fence from the perimeter of his estate. The Scherf estate was protected by the fence and perimeter guards. The brass boxes used by the guards to check in are still visible on the fence line and in the house. After the war, Scherf had the fence rebuilt. (Courtesy of the Scherf family and the City of Andalusia.)

Now that Springdale is owned by the City of Andalusia, it is open for wedding ceremonies and receptions, corporate retreats, school field trips, Easter egg hunts, club meetings, and birthday celebrations. Ruth Aurelia Scherf was married at the First United Methodist Church, but her reception was held here at the Scherf family estate. She later moved with her husband to California. Tragically, J.G. Scherf died of a heart attack after flying out to visit his daughter. (Courtesy of the Scherf family and the City of Andalusia.)

The front doors at Springdale weigh approximately 300 pounds each. Similarly, the doors at the current chamber (the former Alatex office) were also manufactured by Ellison Bronze. The design, first introduced in 1927, is known as "balanced door." J.G. Scherf was one of the first to get his hands on a pair. A full tour including J.G. Scherf family history can be arranged by contacting the City of Andalusia. (Photograph by Denille Spears.)

This historic home, once located at 404 South Three Notch Street, was built in the late 1800s and was purchased in 1905 by Richard Henry Jones. He was an early historian, elected judge, and state solicitor, and also served in the state legislature from 1931 to 1935. (Courtesy of David Walters.)

Built around 1902 for one of Andalusia's first physicians, the Duncan A. McArtan home is a Queen Anne cottage-style residence with a hip and mansard roof covered in slate. It is located at 115 Sixth Avenue behind the First United Methodist Church. It was purchased by McArtan, an influential businessman and banker, in 1904. A family story reports that he was outside instructing the crew to make Sixth Avenue a wide, gracious street when it was being built; they did—and it still is. The McArtan house is one of the oldest homes in the city still occupied by a descendant—granddaughter Lucy Doyle Brady—of original occupants. Her mother owned extensive properties and developed post–World War II McRainey Loop and Doyle Street. (Photograph by Robert Evers.)

The George H. Barnes house is located at 102 Country Club Road. It was constructed in 1939 by Henderson, Black, and Green. The architect was Carl B. Cooper, who also designed Springdale. Barnes partnered with J.G. Scherf as S&B Manufacturing and then went on to work in the Alatex executive office. The home underwent major renovation in 1997 by John Scott Merrill of the Andalusia Development Company. In 2003, another addition was built by George Jr. and Patricia "Sister Schubert" Barnes. Their children and grandchildren are still enjoying the stately residence. (Photograph by Robert Evers.)

This "Country Colonial," built in 1918 at 900 Sanford Road, was constructed on 600 acres of land and given as a wedding gift to Laurin Avant and Olive Elizabeth Crittendon. In 1942, a network of ground observation posts was set up throughout the South and East. A command center was in Montgomery, and Andalusia was picked as a site for an observation post. Mr. and Mrs. Laurin Avant offered their homesite at Sanford Road for use as the post. It was the ideal location away from city lights. This home was fully restored in 1984 by Bill and Teresa Avant. It is listed in the National Register of Historic Places. (Photograph by Denille Spears.)

The Dr. A.M. Richards house was located on South Three Notch Street, across from the Simmons House. It had fluted columns and beautiful beveled-glass side panels with an alluring interior. Dr. Richards was an early physician in Andalusia. The home was later owned by John Grant Wright.

Originally Edwardian, the James Jackson Moates residence was built around 1900 at 300 East Three Notch Street by a Mr. Ballard. The house's brick columns were a later addition. This house is now occupied by Tim Bryan State Farm Insurance office and is the only dwelling more than a century old that is still standing in this area near the square, where homes once lined both sides. J.J. Moates and his wife, Vassie Speller Moates, hosted a dinner reception here for Gov. and Mrs. Bibb Graves in 1928. Moates owned and operated the Victoria Hotel on Pear Street and later started the J.J. Moates Auto Company.

This was at one time owned and occupied by Mr. and Mrs. J.T. Bradshaw and their adopted daughter, Eva Mae, who was later the wife of Count Darling Jr. The home was flanked on the west by the Ashe-Carson Commissary, and on the east side was the home of Judge Robert and Ruth O'Neal Reid. It was located just east of today's Dairy Queen. Mr. Bradshaw was a merchant who also served as sheriff. His wife was a McIntosh and sister of Ms. Prestwood, who lived across the street. (Courtesy of David Walters.)

The J.E. Shreve home, previously located at the present-day site of the Boy Scout Hut, was sold to Henry Opp, who was both the mayor of Andalusia and the attorney responsible for bringing the railroad. His wife lived in this house after his death. Mrs. Opp later married Hill Guy. Mrs. Guy was arguably Andalusia's most fascinating lady. She dined by candlelight, was served by a butler, and was driven by a chauffeur. She eagerly delivered baby gifts to newborns in the area.

The Dr. L.E. Broughton residence was located on East Three Notch across from Springdale. Dr. Ed Broughton and J.T. Brown established the first telephone exchange in Andalusia. Dr. Broughton and his brother, Capt. T.A. Broughton, moved from Greenville, where their father was a physician. Captain Broughton lived in this Edwardian home with his brother until he married Adele Trotter and moved to a house across from Three Notch School, where their son Thomas Ashford Jr. grew up and then attended Marion Military Institute. This house was demolished to make room for the A&P grocery store and, later, Harold's Furniture and Flooring. At one time, the home functioned as a Church of Christ, complete with Eastlake interior finish details and stained-glass windows. The center of the dining room was cut out and replaced with a trapdoor and a pool below for baptism.

Construction started in late 1907 on this Andalusia landmark located at 502 East Three Notch Street. This wood-frame Neoclassical Revival style home was designed by Frank Lockwood. Mr. Shreve was one of the businessmen who gambled on Andalusia and moved with his brothers and family from Searight in 1899, bringing his hardware and feed and seed business to town after the train line was extended. This house has been owned by the Powell, Stokes, and Taylor families. While owned by Hazel Stokes, the house was operated as a tearoom. The home is currently undergoing extensive restoration. (Photograph by Denille Spears.)

The Rankin-Merrill House was built in 1908 on East Three Notch Street by Judge Albert Lamar Rankin and his wife, Addie Hall Randle Rankin, on the west side of today's First Baptist Church. Addie's daughter by her first marriage, Mary Hill Randle, died in the influenza epidemic of 1918. Judge Rankin and Addie's son Albert became an Andalusia attorney and married Carolyn Raborn. E.R. Merrill bought the house from the Rankins. The house had a beautiful staircase, fancy moldings, and parquet floors. Eli's son married Mary Lena Gantt. The Charles Gantt family had the home professionally moved and restored on their estate off Debro Hill, near Montezuma on the Conecuh River. (Courtesy of the Charles Gantt family.)

Located in the J.W. Shreve Historic District, this wood-frame home with slate roof was built in 1906 by Abijah Chapman "A.C." Wilder, a prominent dry goods merchant and lumberman. His dry goods store, Wilder Mercantile, was located on the square in Andalusia and became incorporated in 1911. The Wilder children were Bartlett, Guy, Tracy, Mary, and Cassie. Tracy was mayor of Andalusia, and Polly (daughter of Guy) is married to Sidney Waits, an esteemed Andalusia historian. Roger and Cathy Powell, both renowned local artists, enjoy the vintage ambiance of this residence on Sixth Avenue. (Photograph by Robert Evers.)

Now known as the Cyrus Alfred "C.A." O'Neal Home, this Colonial structure was originally built around 1903 as a public school on the present site of the First Baptist Church sanctuary. A tragic fire destroyed the pine structure on July 31, 1941. The Dixie Division of the National Guard was passing by the home and saw the fire. The men awakened the residents and gave the alarm. A grandfather clock and a grand piano were saved and put out on the lawn. Mrs. O'Neal's diamonds were never found, though the ashes were sifted through for days.

This is the residence of Dr. Thomas Quincy Ray. He is shown here with wife, Nettie, and daughter Quinnie on their front porch of their South Three Notch home place across from the then Foreman's Funeral Home. He was the first chief of staff at the first city hospital a block away. There were two Dr. Rays in Andalusia, and this one was referred to as "Old Dr. Ray." The two were not related.

Among the first elaborate homes to be built in the city of Andalusia was the S.B. "Sump" Milligan home located on South Three Notch Street across from Jack Williams's service station (now a BP station). Several of Andalusia's older citizens place the date of the home in or near the year 1900, because by 1905 the M. Rileys next door had named their first son, Sumpter Riley, after their neighbor. The home had exquisite beveled glass, dark wood finish detail inside, a green Tiffany chandelier, and Queen Anne details inside and out. The dining room had a glazed, raised, Tiffany-style fireplace surround. For many years, Naomi and Ruth Prestwood lived here. At various times, the house has been divided into apartments.

W.F. Simmons, the vice president of First National Bank, and Lela Bell Morgan Simmons, the Andalusia mother selected as Alabama's Mother of the Year on March 29, 1948, and their 10 children lived in this residence at 703 South Three Notch Street. The Victorian home, built around 1906, had seven fireplaces and 14-foot ceilings. Once a fully functioning farm of 22 acres, the property is now located at the center of a bustling neighborhood and occupied by the family of Dr. Steve and Harriet Hubbard, both educators. (Courtesy of Steve and Harriet Hubland.)

This beautiful Colonial home designed by Frank Lockwood was located on East Three Notch Street at the corner of Oak Street. It was built in 1896 as the residence of Anna Chapman Riley and her children after the death of her husband, Judge Malachi Riley. In the 1950s, the structure was moved back from East Three Notch by son John D. Riley, a real estate developer, to allow space for constructing Andalusia Shopping Plaza, the town's first shopping center, anchored by Kwik Chek. This shopping center is currently owned and occupied by Darby's Pharmacy and Cost Plus. Darby's just celebrated the opening of its second pharmacy-and-gift location across the street from Andalusia Regional Hospital.

John Chapman owned extensive properties, including this home and the site that became the present Andalusia High School. In fact, he owned all the property south to East Three Notch Street. As each of his children headed to college, he sold off parts of his farm in lots and blocks. His daughter Anna Claire Chapman Riley lived here. Today, along Second Avenue, pecan trees remain from the Chapman pecan orchard. (Photograph by Robert Evers.)

Recently purchased by Roger LeCompte and Dot Burkett, this house on Church Street was built in 1929 for Dr. Gordon L. Wood. He saw patients in both his home and his office above Thagard Drug Store. The doorways to various downstairs rooms have transoms to allow heat from the coal-burning fireplaces in the living and dining rooms to reach other rooms, and the kitchen and the upstairs had a provision for a stovepipe, presumably for a cookstove for heating the home. All the original interior walls are solid brick, yielding a very sturdy house. The floors in the living room and dining room are oak. The brick walls and the ceiling were finished with plaster, and the rest of the flooring was mostly heart pine. (Courtesy of Roger LeCompte and Dot Burkett.)

This home belonged to George Orkey Waits. Mrs. Waits was a Shaver from the Hubert community and had a collection of antebellum living room furniture, cut glass, and silver that was of museum quality. She had two rare cut-glass lamps in the living room and is remembered for constantly warning young visitors to "watch the cord" for their safety. (Courtesy of David Walters.)

The Pendry home on South Three Notch Street was built in 1922 and is known today as the H. Squire Gillis Sr. Home. Gillis was a local attorney and also a two-term mayor. His wife, Ann Gillis, was a CRNA and sister to Grace Brogden, RN, and Lottie Stanley, RN; all worked at Covington Memorial Hospital, which the Stanleys owned. The building, which once operated as a boardinghouse, has seen dramatic changes to its historic facade through the years. (Photograph by Robert Evers.)

This elegant home at 216 Sixth Avenue was built around 1910 by the Kilpatrick family. Later, it was divided into apartments, but it was restored by Travis and Charlotte Mahone in the 1980s. The stained glass in the porch windows is original to the house. Now owned by the Gaffords, this home is part of the J.W. Shreve Historic District. (Photograph by Robert Evers.)

The Thomas Ashford "T.A." Broughton home was built in 1939 by Capt. "Dash" Broughton. The one-story traditional features floors hewn from hardwood (heart of pine) from a barge that had been submerged in the Conecuh River. The house was designed by architect Carl B. Cooper, who also designed Springdale. This residence was restored and became home to Jones & Jones Law Firm in 1998. J. Fletcher, John F. Jr., and Stacey Bryan Brooks practice law here. Amy Jones currently serves as Covington County circuit clerk. (Photograph by Robert Evers.)

This preserved and restored home is now an office for Goodwyn Mills & Cawood, Inc.; the house was relocated to 207 Church Street. It was once George W. Proctor's family home. The Proctors, including grandson George Harmon Proctor, were very active in the First United Methodist Church. This dwelling was originally located on Dunson Street but was moved to make room for the new *Andalusia Star-News* office building. (Photograph by Robert Evers.)

This was originally a frame house, built before the turn of the century, purchased by A.C. Darling Sr. in 1907. It was extensively renovated in the early 1920s. Frank Lockwood, a well-known architect who designed many of the historic homes in Montgomery, designed the renovations. Mark and Meryane Murphy purchased the house in 1978 and began a long process of restoration the following year. Mark is a third-generation attorney in Andalusia. Meryane, who taught ballet in the front room of the house for several years after it was purchased, is the founder of the Andalusia Ballet. (Photograph by Robert Evers.)

The Monch Riley Home, also known as the McEachin Home, was restored and converted into law offices by attorney John Peek. Riley was a barkeeper and saloon operator. The house once had beautiful stained-glass windows, and the dining room chandelier was unique, with two white tear-shaped gloves that hung down. Riley's daughter married a McEachin, and they resided in the home after Riley's death. When the McEachins moved to Enterprise, Jess Dixon bought the house. His daughter-in-law (the first wife of Julian Dixon) had a beauty shop here. (Photograph by Robert Evers.)

The Wilkes Home was built around 1910 at 700 South Three Notch Street. This historic Victorian located at the top of Bay Branch Hill was occupied by some of Andalusia's most well-known families, including those of George Adams (formerly of the Frank-Stewart house), George Barnes (later built on Country Club Road), Hugh Broadhurst (military retiree who became president of First Federal), and Claud Clark (Mrs. Clark was a Simmons and grew up in the Simmons house across the street), and was purchased by third-generation hardware mogul "Uncle Bob" and Denise Brooks, in the 1980s. (Photograph by Robert Evers.)

Sears, Roebuck and Co. mail-order homes were originally shipped by rail to Andalusia to fill the need for the numerous employees from Chicago to work at Swift Packing Company. Everything one needed to construct these homes could be selected and ordered by catalog, shipped in a package by train, and put together by hand. This home at 515 South Three Notch Street belonged to Dr. Richard Kearley. His veterinary clinic was behind the house. Kearley played football at Auburn, and hanging from a light in his clinic were the football and cleats from a big win there. He also coached the first Andalusia High School football team. (Courtesy of Sue Bass Wilson.)

This is the Sumpter B. Milligan home on the corner of East Three Notch Street and Second Avenue. Milligan was the president of FNBB. His daughter Cecilia married James Earl McGowin, and the interior wood came from McGowin Lumber Company in Chapman. His son, also named Sumpter, married Ruby Law of the Henry Law House; but he died of tuberculosis, and there were no children. What is now St. Mary's Episcopal Church in Andalusia started in this house, with meetings held in the former music room. The Milligans had come up from Milton, Florida, where they are now buried. (Photograph by Robert Evers.)

The C.B. Mathews House was built in the 1920s and is located in the J.W. Shreve Historic District. Mathews was in the lumber and turpentine business. The foyer was furnished with exquisite carved Chinese teakwood furniture that the Mathewses bought on their honeymoon. Mrs. Mathews owned two other houses on the property, including the one behind this home that she built for her daughter Gladys. When Gladys married, Mrs. Mathews operated a rooming house, known as the Mathews House, here. Olan Mills, the photographer, would stay in a room upstairs and set up his equipment in the living room, using it as his temporary studio. The family still has a series of portrait photographs that were taken and signed by Mills. He would bring outfits along with him for his photo shoots, so his subjects could dress up as cowboys and Indians, for example. (Photograph by Robert Evers.)

Snead House was built around 1904 at 218 Stanley Avenue. Judge Snead and his family lived there until 1935, when it was purchased by Aubrey Mallette, a druggist who reared his family in the home for more than 50 years. It is currently owned by Randy and Kym Keahey, who operate Keahey Funeral Home next door. (Photograph by Robert Evers.)

The W.C. Merrill home was built in the 1930s for the owner of Andalusia Manufacturing Company. Many of the historic homes still standing on Three Notch Street and in the J.W. Shreve Historic District were built by Merrill. Charlie and Marge Bass occupied this residence for 43 years, in which time they raised their four children. Their youngest child, Tripp, and his wife, Regina, purchased the historic home in 2007. Tripp and Regina have since raised their own three children in the home. Brother and sister Tripp Bass and Sue Bass Wilson serve the real estate needs of Covington County through their family-owned business, Bass Agency Real Estate. Their father, Charlie, opened the business in 1946. (Photograph by Robert Evers.)

The T.A. Patrick home was built in 1908 by Preston and Lena (Dunson) Gantt on South Three Notch Street. Preston was a lumber merchant and superintendent of shipping for the Frierson Mills, and he farmed 1,200 acres. Thomas Arthur Patrick was the second owner of the home. He came to Andalusia in 1901 and opened a bicycle, hardware, and furniture store. He married Laura Bonner in 1905, and they purchased this home after a fire destroyed their residence on Sanford Road. In 2008, the house was purchased by Chad and Kerry Alexander, who opened Alexander Electric and Alexander Properties, LLC, in 2010. (Photograph by Robert Evers.)

Six

TRANSPORTATION AND THE FLOOD OF 1929

Timber was very important in this area during the late 1890s. Primitive tools facilitated this job before the train revolutionized the industry. Back then, only about one in four trees was fit for rafting down the river. When people moved into the area wanting to farm, they had a lot of clearing to do.

This old postcard from South Three Notch Street shows the standard modes of travel during the early 1900s. The horse and buggy belonged to Leolive Henderson. Sidewalks were added in the early 1920s when the main streets were paved.

Most farmers and families used a mule and wagon to go into town once a week for sugar, flour, tools, and other notions. These trips were usually made on Saturdays. Only the most well-to-do families had access to horse-drawn buggies. The courthouse, the town bakery, hardware stores, clothing stores, and cafés were all open on Saturdays. Most businesses closed on Thursday afternoons back then.

Ben and Billy Ray of Birmingham rode these ponies from their home in North Alabama to Andalusia to deliver them to Dr. T.Q. Ray (their grandfather's farm). Many families had chicken houses, vegetable gardens, cows, horses, donkeys, oxen-pulled buggies, wagons, and carriages.

For those who could not afford their own horse and buggy, they could be hired at the Shreve Milligan Livestock and Vehicle Company. Many a Sunday-afternoon buggy ride was enjoyed especially by those a'courting!

Pictured here is Ruth Scherf, wife of Mayor J.G. Scherf. She had her own car. The first automobile, or "gasoline buggy," came to Andalusia after being purchased by Charles J. Ward in Atlanta. It was the first model Oldsmobile built. Ward operated a bicycle shop in Andalusia and was in Atlanta to buy bicycles. The car was shipped to Andalusia by train, and people lined up at the train station to see his purchase.

W.A. Riley Transfer was a for-hire business used to move people and parcels around as needed. For most, a horse and buggy or a wagon would suffice, but for larger packages or longer distances a transfer service was the most efficient mode of transportation. Most country roads were dirt paths with two ruts worn by wagon wheels and a grassy strip in the middle. These roads were often hard and bumpy; in warm months, they were dry and dusty, while in the spring they were wet and muddy. It took several days to travel north to Montgomery.

Only the wealthiest families could afford to own and maintain their own automobile. Therefore, the family of these girls has hired W.A. Riley Transfer to transport them from Andalusia to Birmingham. Based on road conditions, travel was both difficult and expensive. Most roads were so narrow that if two buggies met, one might be forced into a ditch along the side of the road. There were few bridges in those days, so drivers simply drove their wagons through rivers and streams.

This is part of the Horse Shoe Lumber Company after the first tracks were laid in the area. Before the train track crossed this countryside, early settlers built their homes out of logs. They sometimes used the whole, round log, and other times they would square them up with hand tools. Most homes were one or two-room affairs, and it was not uncommon for four or five people to sleep in the same room.

This early Central of Georgia steam locomotive is pulling a log train on a wye in Andalusia just after the turn of the century. In the late 1890s, business leaders in Andalusia posted a $5,000 prize for the first rail line to pass through the town. The Central of Georgia Railway claimed the prize, completing the track in September 1899, and built a depot on land donated by residents. The town flourished with the new rail connection; the population rose from 551 in 1900 to 2,480 in 1910. The Central of Georgia Depot in Andalusia has since been restored and converted into the Three Notch Museum.

This is a Pole Road Locomotive, built by Tanner & Delaney, Shop No. 1657, around 1887. This model is called Goliath. The boiler is made of the best selected homogeneous steel plates and was thoroughly tested to carry high pressure. The framework of wrought-iron and steel is very substantial and heavy. The driving wheels are 30 inches in diameter on the tread, and each of them is driven separately by a chain with a breaking strain of over 12 tons. The engine shaft, master shaft, and axles are all of the best steel. A first-class governor controls the speed of the engine—about five miles per hour.

At its zenith, the Louisville & Nashville (L&N) was a 6,000-mile railroad system that served 13 states. The railroad was economically strong throughout its lifetime, operating both freight and passenger trains in a manner that earned it the nickname, "The Old Reliable." The L&N depot in Andalusia is pictured here. The L&N Railroad ran a line from Georgiana through Andalusia and Opp to Graceville, Florida. (Photograph by Denille Spears.)

Businesses flourished as the advent of rail transportation spurred the growth of Andalusia from a small rural county seat to a regional supplier of wholesale goods to surrounding towns and communities and a regional market point of shipment for locally produced raw materials. This progress also brought better roadways and affordable automobiles and meant that there was less of a need for passenger trains in the South. Passenger train service in Andalusia was discontinued around 1945. Court documents show that the Alabama Public Service Commission sued the L&N Railroad Company to force it to continue the service. Litigation was pending in US district court for years. Currently, this passenger car is one of the artifacts that remains. (Photograph by Denille Spears.)

Evers Furniture staff members are seen unloading cargo from train to trucks of new shipments of Norges refrigerators. Pictured in front are L.H. Evers and Comer Evers. Around 1938 or 1939, L.H. built a two-story building on Church Street to accommodate his furniture business, which featured route trucks transporting furniture from showroom to the homes.

The Horse Shoe Lumber Company mill at River Falls included River Falls Power and the Point "A" and Gantt Dams on the Conecuh River. The flood of 1929 was the worst disaster yet recorded to hit this area. It began raining continuously on Monday, March 10, 1929, flooding the mill and severely damaging Gantt and Point "A." No lumber was ever produced at this site afterwards.

By Tuesday night, March 11, 1929, the streams were flooding. Power plants at River Falls, Point "A," and Gantt, from which Andalusia, Opp, and several other towns and cities received their electrical power, were flooded. Turbines and generators at these hydroelectric plants were stilled. All homes and business establishments were in the dark. The planer mill, where lumber was finished and shipped out, also flooded. Pictured in the background to the right is the office of the Horse Shoe Lumber Company.

The rains continued, the lightning flashed, and the thunder roared. Water washed over bridges and highways. Lowlands were deep underwater. Up and down these streams, residents were forced to leave their homes. Many of them lost their livestock, feed stuffs, and home furnishings in the swift waters. This is the railroad crossing at the "Brickyard" and Pickle Plant Crossing. On the left is the brickyard, and on the right are the pickling vats. The road is just to the right of the pine tree. (Courtesy of David Walters.)

Onlookers are pictured evaluating the damage to the highway bridge and the trestle at Gantt after the water began to recede. The other end of the trestle was completely washed out.

The continuous rain had caused the spillways of two power plants to blow out from the water pressure. Complete sections were washed away. Damage assessment could not be done until the waters began to recede on Sunday, March 17, 1929.

The old River Falls bridge can be seen in the background after the flood. In the foreground on the right are the remains of Warden Crawford's house. E.L. More's barn is crumpled up against it. On the left is Mrs. Maynard Padgett's house.

Damage to the tracks and the Horse Shoe Lumber Company is visible in this photograph, taken after the floodwater receded. The planer mill is in the center background, and the sawmill is at right.

The town of River Falls was inundated, and its occupants were evacuated. The highest points in that area, which had never been flooded before, were now several feet underwater. This is Leonard Hart's house in River Falls, pictured before the flood.

Leonard Hart's home is pictured after the devastating flood. Andalusia residents rushed to help provide clothes, shelter, and food to those affected most by the storms. Charlie Brunson, owner of the Andalusia Bakery, waded across a shallow spot, delivering bread to Charlie Sellers, owner of the Red Level store, daily until the water receded.

So many families and businesses were lost in the flood. This barn was found upside down. Tenacity was found locally, and many chose to rebuild.

Another home was damaged and displaced by the flood. On higher ground in Andalusia, water came up over the dirt road that passed near the pond. Sidney Waits remembers his father letting him ride on the running board of the car so he could drag his foot in the water as his dad drove through it—and he didn't have to wash his feet that night!

Here is another view of the damage done at the highway bridge and the trestle at Gantt while water was still rising. The trestles ended up being completely washed out. (Courtesy of David Walters.)

Seven

INDUSTRY AND COMMERCE

In 1923, Covington County's largest industry and the nation's third-largest shirt manufacturing industry began its operation. The first operation was begun in the old First Methodist Church on Church Street. J.G. Scherf named the operation Andala, for Andalusia and Alabama. It grew from seven plants in 1923 with an annual payroll of $25,000 to a payroll of $14 million in 1972. A second company, Alabama Textile Products Corporation, was begun in March 1929 in a building on the west side of town that formerly operated as Swift & Company's meatpacking plant. George H. Barnes and several other people moved to Andalusia from South Norwalk, Connecticut, to assist with the training of operators and installation of quality standards.

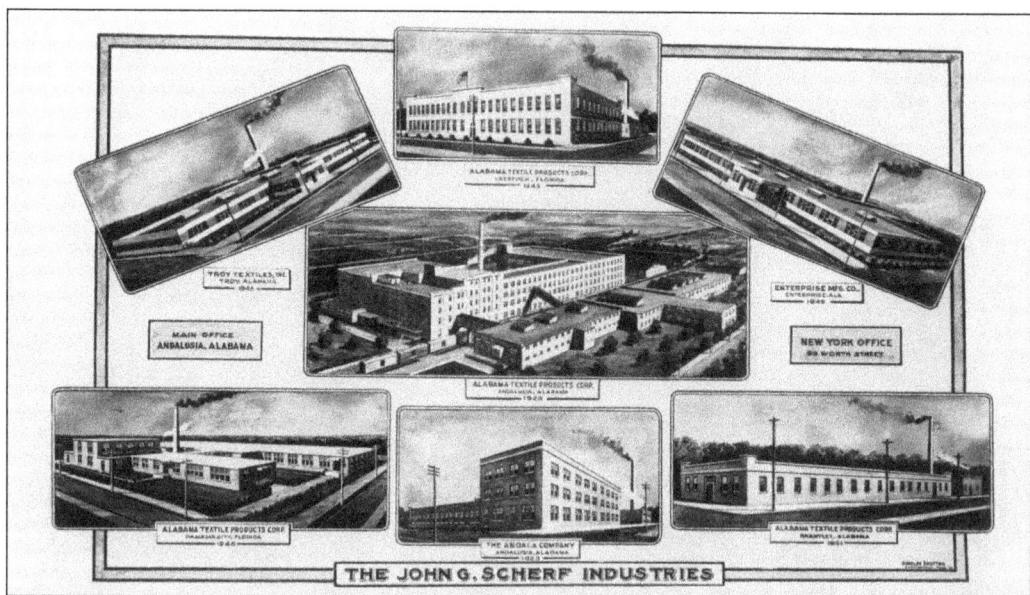

THE JOHN G. SCHERF INDUSTRIES

John G. Scherf Industries operated the following textile corporations: the Andala Company (Andalusia, Alabama); Alabama Textile Products Corp. (Andalusia and Brantley, Alabama; and Crestview and Panama City, Florida); Troy Textiles, Inc. (Troy, Alabama); and Enterprise Manufacturing Company (Enterprise, Alabama).

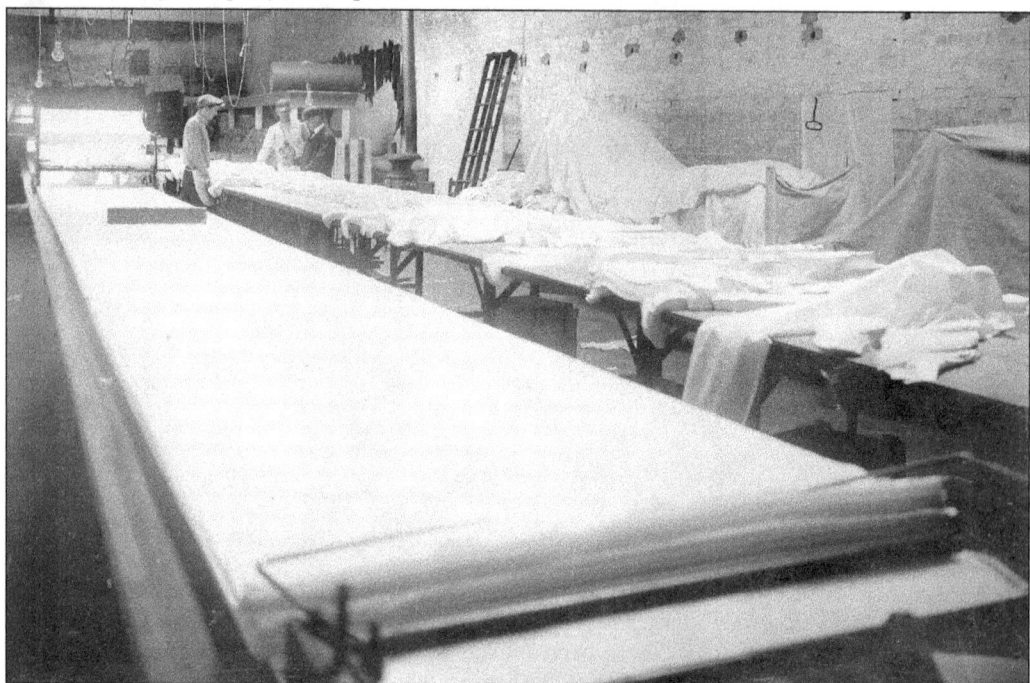

The long roll of fabric is visible on the left of the cloth room. On the right table are the shirt pattern pieces already cut. These would be moved to another area for assembly. In 1933, the Andalusia plant began production of men's shirts for Arrow, and production eventually grew to a large volume. A rough estimate of the number of Arrow dress shirts manufactured by Alatex and its affiliates from 1929 to 1952 would be in excess of four million dozen.

Women are working at industrial sewing machines on the second floor, piecing garments together. On the bottom floor, on the left there are more rows of industrial machines and stacks of completed garments and pieces ready to become shirts. In addition to shirts, Alatex and its affiliates manufactured more than 2.5 million dozen of Arrow dress shorts between 1933 and 1952.

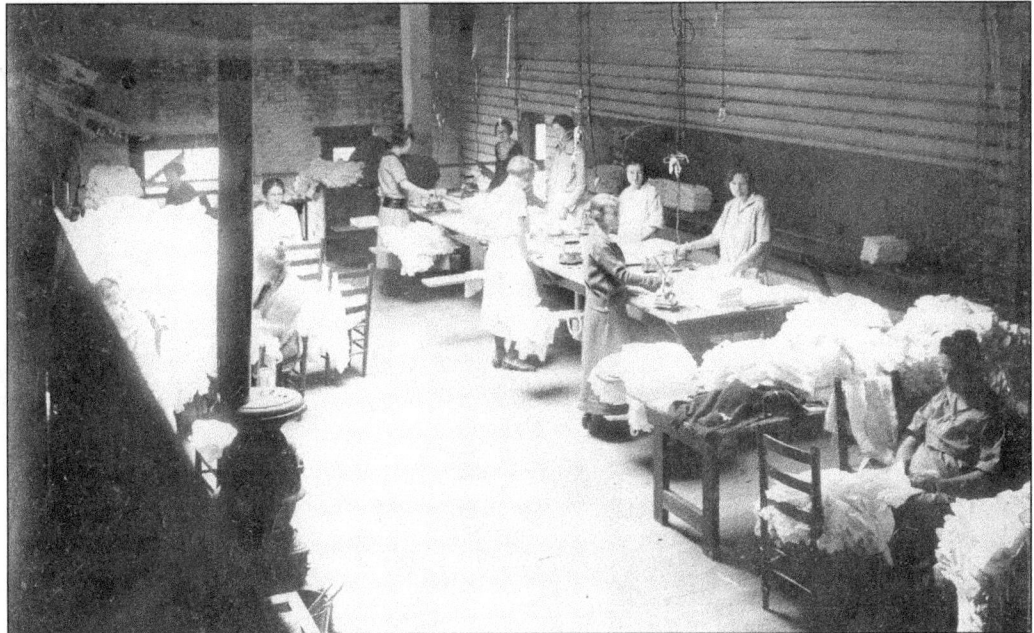

The pressing room of the Andala plant is shown here in 1923, with men's underwear and shirts being pressed. In the beginning, the plant only manufactured underwear, but in later years it added work shirts and pants for Sears, Roebuck and Co.

In the inspection room, cloth would have been inspected to be sure it met the National Textile Association's guidelines for thread-count quality. In 1933, the Andalusia plant began production of men's shirts for Arrow. Production grew, according to the company's 15-year appreciation program, "from a relatively small operation to a plant with an annual output of approximately four million shirts and three million shorts—enough to 'dress up' every man in all of the southern states."

The Andala was a prominent place that most women could find dependable employment. It is impossible to count the vast numbers that helped support their families through this employer. The new chamber of commerce office is located in the renovated and restored Alatex headquarters. Many photographs of these devoted employees are on display there.

The first drugstore in Andalusia was owned by J.D. McPherson. A wooden structure about where Turner's Fine Apparel was located, it is now the office of attorney Wayne Bush. In 1902, A.M. Riley, a graduate of Howard College, bought one-half interest in the drug firm from McPherson. This was one of the most popular spots when Dr. Sentell built the first brick building on the square in 1904. Riley bought McPherson's interest and in 1908 moved into the new brick location on the south corner of the J.A. Prestwood block. Riley continued to operate this business until his death around 1938. Riley is pictured on the left. The other employees in this 1938 photograph are unidentified.

When the railroads came to Andalusia in 1898, Captain Broughton opened a drugstore called Brown & Broughton Druggists on the square. According to a 1905 fire map, behind it was located the first telephone exchange. The first local gaslights were used in this store, and many walk-in customers enjoyed chocolate malts served here.

In 1914, Matt and Charlie Brunson, sons of M.E. Brunson, opened Andalusia's first bakery and one of the earliest such enterprises in South Alabama. Their father and mother had been in the hotel business for about 10 years, when the Brunson brothers became master bakers in their own right. Around 1920 or 1921, Charlie and Matt purchased the bakery from their father and moved the operation across the street to get above ground level. The health department started inspections about that time, and the brothers found it both necessary to move aboveground and important to get in full view of the public to increase their business. Matt eventually moved to Texas, joining his other brothers. Charlie was the only one of the 12 Brunson children to remain in Andalusia. Pictured from left to right are Ellie "Buddy" Brunson, L. Pruitt, Ingram Williams, Charlie Brunson Sr., and M.E. Brunson Jr. (Courtesy of Sue Bass Wilson.)

In 1944, the Brunson Bakery moved from South Cotton Street to the Payne building on 200 South Three Notch Street across from the City Drug Store. With this move, a certain amount of automation was introduced, including a revolving oven that baked 1,242 loaves of bread every 45 minutes (four times faster than the old method). The company's bread was known as Bluebird Bread. In the early 1950s, the bakery acquired its first bread-slicing and wrapping machine. Daughter Carolyn Brunson artistically and masterfully decorated thousands of birthday and wedding cakes. (Courtesy of Sue Bass Wilson.)

82

The first hospital was the Covington Hospital on South Three Notch Street. It was in a converted home. The old home had a wraparound porch with lots of filigree and dentil work on its facade. It was organized and incorporated in 1918. Dr. Quincy Ray was the staff physician at this hospital. (Courtesy of David Walters.)

Here, patients wait to see Dr. Juanita McDonald, Andalusia's first female doctor. "Dr. Mac" enjoyed an enviable practice and maintained a small clinic at the intersection of East Three Notch and College Streets after first practicing at a Dunson Street location. (Courtesy of Andalusia Public Library.)

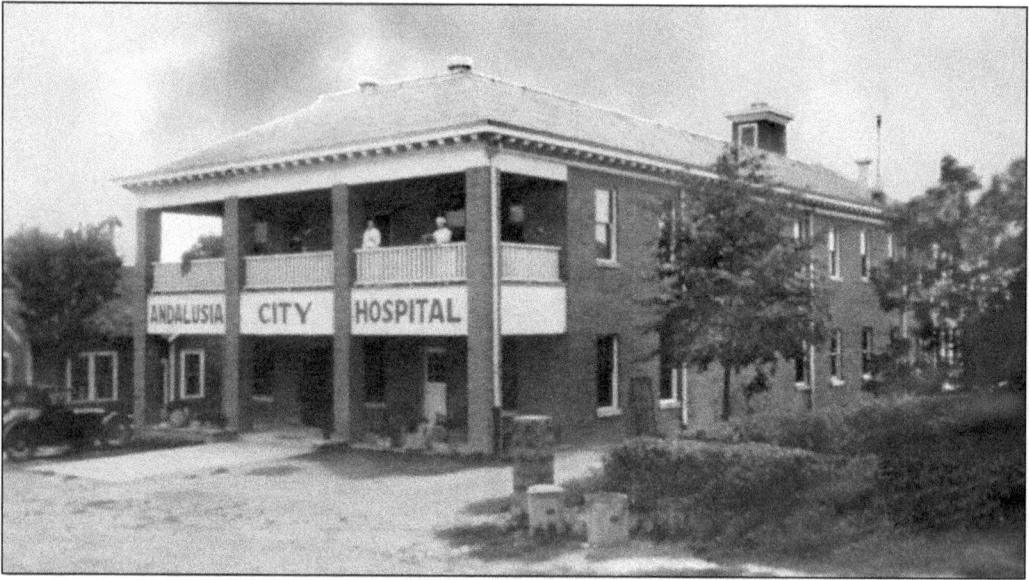

The Andalusia City Hospital became the Covington Memorial Hospital, owned by the Stanley family. The building, located on the southeast corner at the intersection of South Cotton and Watson Streets, was removed during the 1960s.

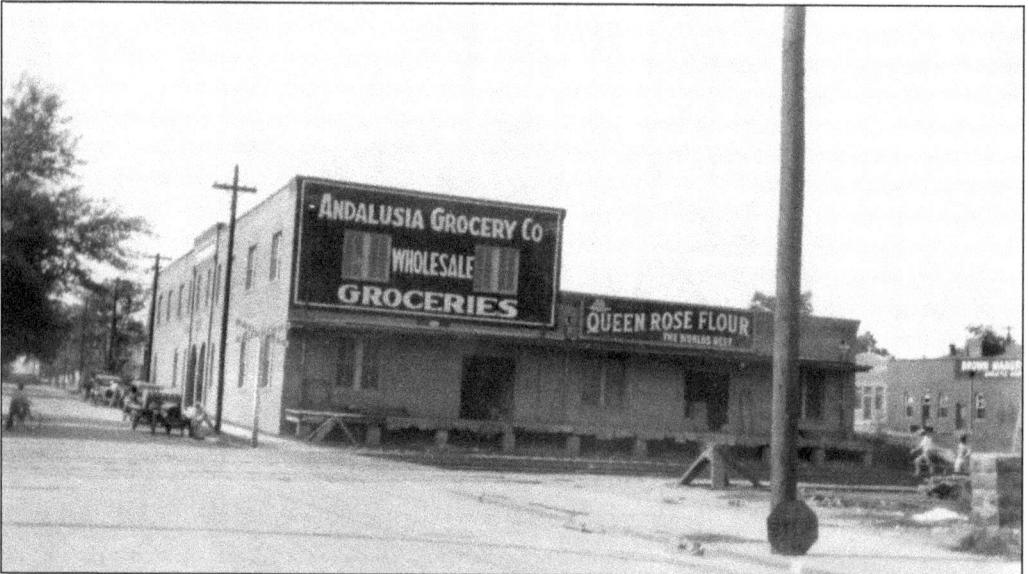

Andalusia Grocery Company was located at the corner of South Cotton Street and Jernigan Street, just across from the L&N Railroad Depot. Owned by A.C. Wilder, E.D. Lorraine, and William Thweatt in 1919, this wholesale grocery business was used for storage and commodities.

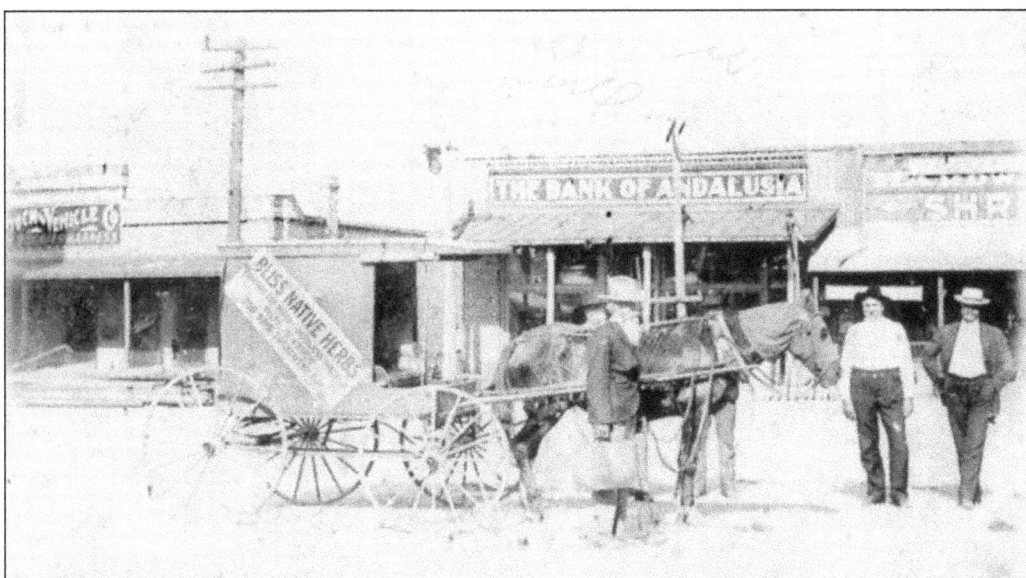

The Bank of Andalusia on the northeast public square was organized in 1904 to provide an alternative to the existing First National Bank of Andalusia. It opened with capital stock of $50,000. The organizers of the Bank of Andalusia arrived with the railroads in 1899. By 1914, the bank's capital had grown to $100,000, and the organizers decided to build their own location. Cyrus A. O'Neal and E.L. More (who were partners in the Horse Shoe Lumber Company and the River Falls Power Plant) acquired a controlling interest, increased stock to $200,000, and renamed the bank the Andalusia National Bank. By 1924, a two-story addition was made to the back of the bank. Later, the building was also home to the Commercial Bank and Covington County Bank.

Benson Hardware was originally located on the east side of the square. The door to the extreme left led through to the Bank of Andalusia and the newspaper office. It was a one-story building, but in later years, a second story was added. It was later located on Central Street just north of the C of G Depot. The hardware store embalmed bodies in the back and sold caskets before the funeral home business was established in the late 1930s.

Andalusia and Covington County started out with an agriculturally based economy. The textile industry changed some of that way of life. The Benson house is shown here on the left. "Miss Pinkie's" well was known to have fine cold water. When she sold the property to A.C. Darling, for him to locate his car dealership here, it was with the stipulation that her well not be covered up. It still exists today on the corner of East Three Notch and Central Streets.

According to the *Andalusia Times* of June 19, 1908, "A delightful time was had Monday evening at Guice's Tomato Farm, when ice cold tomatoes and peaches were enjoyed by the following couples: P. Lewis and Miss Martha Riley, Captain Broughton and Miss Adele Trotter; Dr. Gresham and Miss Dawson of Montgomery; N. A. McMillan and Miss Fannie Lou Riley; R.A. Parks and Miss Carol Perrenot, and Mr. & Mrs. Z.D. Studstill."

Andalusia's Foundry and Machine Shop was used to make farm implements, outhouse privy toilet seats, timber tools, and any gadgets necessary to keep the South moving forward. On market days, multiple vendors sold their wares at the foundry.

The Andalusia (Ford) Motor Company was located in the Fletcher Building on Church Street. This business started by Howard Ward was known for many years as the "oldest Ford dealer in Alabama." This early location is the present site of the Andalusia Fire Department. The dealership, later owned by Ward's son-in-law Luther Tayor Jr., was the first auto sales business to locate on the then new bypass in 1968. Andalusia Ford is still a vital part of Andalusia's business community. Hunter Owen and family have been serving the automotive needs of the area for more than 20 years.

This 1910 image of the Prestwood Building shows a business center featuring, from left to right, the A.M. Riley Drug Store; a movie house owned by Z.D. Studstill; a millinery owned by Mrs. G.A. Kilpatrick and Frank Shaver's Store. The movie house was the scene of a movie filmed in the early 1900s. Few people remember much about it, except that it was actually filmed in Andalusia and that the following people either acted in it or were associated with it: Cleve Bean, John D. Riley, and W.L. Padgett.

The Shreve & Milligan Livestock and Vehicle Company was available for carriage, buggy, or mules for hire, for residents or visitors. It is one of the oldest businesses in Andalusia, dating back to the 1890s. A second story was eventually added. Later known as the Milligan Building (since the Shreves constructed another building on North Cotton Street), it is occupied by the Murphy & Murphy Law Firm today.

O'Neal, Law & Co. Horses, Mules, Buggies, Wagons was located to the west of the First Baptist Church. After being shipped to Andalusia on the Central of Georgia train, mules were unloaded and driven around the square to O'Neal stables. This short street was shown on old maps as North Three Notch Street and is now known as O'Neal Court.

Inside Wilder's Store in the Prestwood Building, customers could find ready help from (pictured from left to right) G.W. Moye, Guy B. Wilder Sr., Burie Parrish, and Simon Rayborn. The store offered dry goods, boots, shoes, and dress goods while also offering staples like bacon, lard, flour, sugar, coffee, corn, oats, and bran.

Tisdale & Brooks Hardware & Furniture was established in 1913 by Bob Tisdale and S.D. Brooks. Tisdale Brooks, son of S.D. Brooks, purchased the store in 1945 after returning from World War II. In this undated photograph, a large crowd has gathered, waiting for the store to open.

Bob Brooks purchased the store from his father in 1975 and moved into its current location on South Three Notch in 1976. Today, Brooks Hardware is still family owned. Daughter Emily Brooks Crowson and son-in-law Nick Crowson are now raising the fourth generation of hardware enthusiasts. They have also added a new toy department offering hard-to-find toy collectibles and everyday gifts. Hardware and farming artifacts from the old days are displayed inside, and some antique collectibles are for sale. (Photograph by Robert Evers.)

This is Columbia General Hospital on Hillcrest Drive. Built by Dr. Ray Evers, the hospital was eventually torn down to make way for the Covington County Administration Building, which houses the newly reelected for a third term Sheriff Dennis Meeks and the Covington County Sheriff's Department as well as Covington County Commission offices. The Covington County Jail is adjacent on the south side..

Doctors and volunteers donated their time and services to care for the poor or needy through the Crippled Children's Clinic held at the Scherf Memorial Building on Opp Avenue. Local civic organizations like the Parnassus Club and the Mentor Club (now Coterie) helped staff the program, and the J.G. Scherf Foundation helped provide financial backing.

This is a c. 1908 sketch of the McArtan Opera House. In the bottom-right corner was located the Moore-Dozier Drug Store (later the City Drug Store). The Opera House was the center for the arts during this era. Traveling entertainment such as magicians, soloists, and theater groups often performed here. Graduation and piano recitals were staged in this three-story facility prior to the construction of the East Three Notch School and auditorium. The building was gutted by fire around 1915.

The old Paramount opened on July 7, 1935, with Mae West's *Goin' to Town*. It was first located in the building later occupied by Turner's Store. The other picture show, Fox Theatre, operated mostly on Fridays and Saturdays and was located on East Three Notch Street at the corner of Central Street. The weekend serials were a must. Missing one was almost considered a sin. Admission back then was 10¢ and 15¢. Z.D. Studstill was owner of these two theaters, and Julian Studstill was in charge of the projection booths. Back then, films were highly flammable. At least two projection-booth fires were recorded. Fortunately, no one was seriously injured.

Shoes were made and repaired in shops like this. Pictured here in the 1920s are C.L. Northcutt, owner; Robert Braxton; and W.R. Brooks, who later founded Brooks Shoe Shop on South Three Notch Street. The Brooks Shoe Shop still operates in the same location today.

Brooks Shoe Shop is still serving Andalusia in the same location, right off the square. Hilry (pictured) and Betty Trawick are the owners. (Photograph by Robert Evers.)

Inside this Cadillac dealership, a customer got a glimpse of the most modern vehicles available at the time. This was the Studstill-Mathews Cadillac car dealership. It was located on the north side of East Three Notch Street where WAAO and Patel and Sledge Law Firm are located. It was built by Trammel Henderson, bank president.

The Cadillac dealership was a popular dealership, but a disagreement led to new ownership. The current building is decorated with a mural depicting a legend of Andalusia, as told by attorney James Prestwood. Across the street, the historical marker on the corner of Three Notch and Central memorializes the Three Notch Trail on one side and the locale of Hank and Audrey Williams' wedding site on the other.

The Coca-Cola Bottling Company was brought to Andalusia by the Walter Bellingrath family of Mobile. "Mamie" Elizabeth Bellingrath Burnette, owner of the Coca-Cola franchise for the South Alabama region, moved to Andalusia along with her husband, George Burnette, who managed the business. This photograph shows a school group at the facility to take a tour. The ice plant and cold storage facility was also here.

Wiley Kilpatrick, born and raised in Heath, went to work with W.R. Tisdale as a bookkeeper. When Tisdale's health failed him, Wiley and his brother-in law, Marvin Mashburn, bought the mercantile establishment of W.R. Tisdale and did business as Kilpatrick & Mashburn for a number of years. Kilpatrick died at the age of 51 after suffering a stroke. This is another photograph of a booming square. (Courtesy of David Walters.)

Christo's 5 and 10 Cent Stores appeared around the 1940s. This one was located in the building on the south side of the public square. The smell of popcorn filled the air of this well-known dime store. It was a popular place for young teens to frequent on Saturdays, especially the girls, who could pick from a plethora of lipsticks and necklaces.

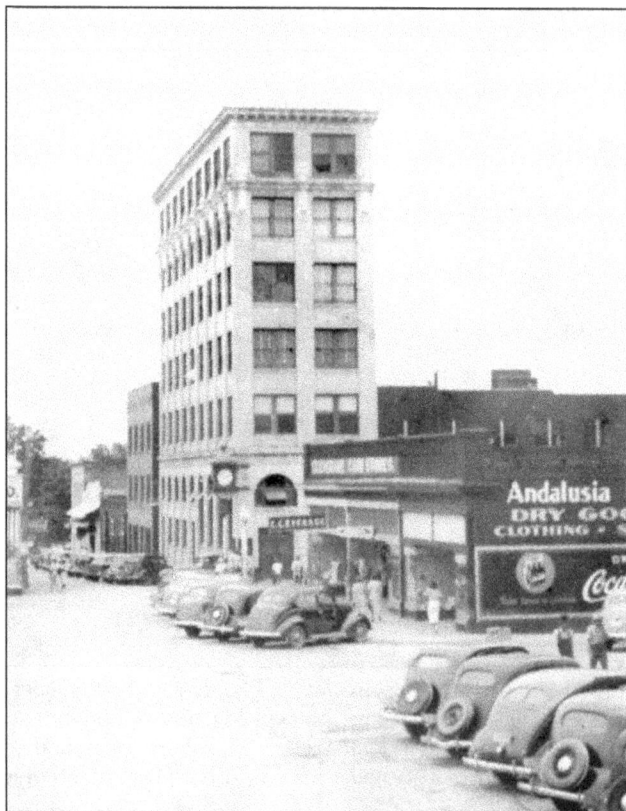

Andalusia's tallest building, the First National Bank Building, was constructed in 1921. It merged with Andalusia National Bank in 1931 and closed due to insolvency in 1932. The First National Bank Building was fully occupied by tenants when the landmark clock was installed. Recently, this iconic clock was adopted as the new Andalusia Area Chamber of Commerce logo (designed by Robert Evers). Later purchased by Frank Timmerman, owner of an insurance business, the building became known as the Timmerman Building. Listed in the National Register of Historic Places, it was designed by architect Frank Lockwood. Just like the courthouse, it was built by Little and Cleckers of Anniston.

The Bank of Andalusia built this stylish yet sturdy structure on the square in 1904. The bank was purchased by E.L. More and C.A. O'Neal, partners in the Horse Shoe Lumber Company, and converted to the Andalusia National Bank. The structure also housed Andalusia Jewelry Company and Covington County Bank. It was restored and occupied by attorney Sidney Fuller until his death in 2012 and is now occupied by attorney John Peek.

Hudson Motor Car Company was founded by auto pioneers Howard Coffin, George W. Dunham, and Roy E. Chapin, and largely funded by department store owner Joseph L. Hudson. In 1910, just one year after it was created, Hudson was the 11th-largest auto company in America—a country then rife with automakers. Andalusia was no different and became home to more than 30 automobile dealerships through the years. The building for this original Hudson dealership in Andalusia is still partially standing across from the public library on South Three Notch Street. In later years, it became Moates Garage.

The Green Mill, named after the long-standing jazz club located in Chicago's Uptown neighborhood that opened in 1907, became a popular hangout for area residents. In the 1920s, the Chicago location gained infamy as a hangout for mobsters. (Courtesy of David Walters.)

Jim Taylor, probably rated one of the best garage men in the state, was district gin manager of the Southern Cotton Oil Company. He was employed by this company for five months in the fall and operated the Prestwood Gin during the ginning season. Taylor, an expert on machinery, opened a repair shop in a two-story wooden building in 1909. He then moved into a brick building where the courthouse now stands. Partnering with John Fletcher, an authorized dealer of Buicks, he moved into this building in 1910. It later was T-P Flower and Gift Shop, owned by the Taylor and Pippin families, before becoming Juliann's. Today, Pirate Graphics proudly calls this building home. The structure is decorated with several murals, including the one commemorating the justice-of-the-peace wedding of Hank and Audrey Williams.

Moates Garage, operated by J.J. Moates on South Three Notch, offered washing and polishing, full-service repair work, and oil changes. This building is still partially standing.

This is the interior of Moates Garage, which stood ready to offer services or parts as needed, including a huge selection of tires.

Andalusia's Dime Taxi is pictured here in the late 1930s. From left to right are Red Mancil, Dick Ward (uncle of Von Polson), and an unidentified man. This photograph was taken on the square, with Covington Stores (the Milligan Building) in the background. Franklin Taxicab Company followed the Dime Taxi business. It was headquartered on South Cotton Street.

Owner Jonas Hair (right) and staff prepare to meet customers to take in clothes to be laundered. They also offered hat cleaning and blocking, which consists of completely disassembling the hat carefully and cautiously by hand. The sweatband; lining; hatband; and additional trimmings, such as feathers, hatpins, and embellishments, are removed from the hat. Once the hat is disassembled, the master hatter proceeds to carefully hand wash all parts of the hat, completely removing any stains, spots, and smells the hat has acquired. Then all parts of the hat are placed in the drying room, where natural sunlight is used to remove the condensation from the hat before it is stretched over a wooden hat block, creating the correct size before it is reassembled.

According to the Insurance Fire map of 1905, Star Cleaners was under construction at the time the map was drawn. Notice that the building advertises Star Cleaners as the oldest in Andalusia. Indeed, when phone service was first extended, one needed only to dial "5" to reach the cleaners!

Inside Star Cleaners, Herman J. Hair is pictured working in the back, where the wash process was first started.

This Andalusia service station was owned and operated by the Lidh family at their East Three Notch location and offered complete service for most vehicles. It was one of the many dealerships trying to bring gas-powered automobiles to Covington County.

This H-C Sinclair station was opened by G.S. Waits Sr. as Covington County's first drive-in service station with curbside service in 1924. Hank Williams often played at the old River Side Inn on the banks of the Conecuh in River Falls, and he was married right here in Andalusia. A record of his marriage license is on file at the local probate judge's office. In 1944, Justice of the Peace Boyette performed the ceremony in this very service station. Hank also had his appendix removed at the local hospital by Dr. Ray Evers.

The Martin Theatre chain opened in Andalusia in October 1940. It opened with "Magic Doors" and a "Magic Eye" drinking fountain. These two innovations were certainly new and created quite a stir. As people approached the doors, they automatically opened and remained open until one could enter the theater vestibule. To drink from the water fountain, patrons would simply bend over the spout to cause the water to automatically begin to flow. This venue is also believed to have shown the first talking movies in Andalusia.

Residents complained that inflation had raised the movie prices from 10¢ to 25¢ at the Martin Theatre with the introduction of talking films. By the 1950s, the Martin Theatre had become the most popular place for children to spend a Saturday afternoon, viewing such films as The Blob, The Incredible Shrinking Man, and the unforgettable 3-D movie House of Wax. The Sunday matinee was also well attended.

The J.C. Penney Company moved into small towns around the states between 1913 and 1924, arriving in Andalusia around 1929. J.C. Penney is Andalusia's longest-surviving national chain store. Today, it is located in the Covington Mall. The storefront on South Three Notch Street is pictured here.

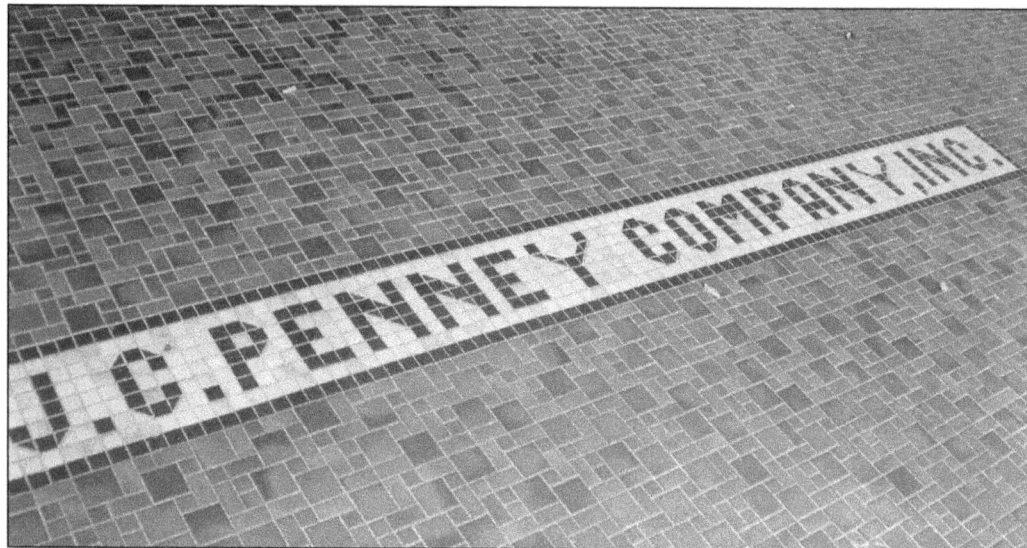

An exciting architectural detail that can be found on some of the historic structures in Andalusia is decorative tile spelling out the store name. Other structures, like the Bass-Tipler Building, had a cornerstone with the name carved in stone. The Evers Furniture store also had decorative tile at the entrance.

First home to the Adams family, then the Robert O'Neal family, this Victorian residence was converted for use by Foreman Funeral Home, founded on April 1, 1938, by Emmette Max Foreman. In 1953, the Foremans' daughter and son-in-law joined the firm. In 1962, Foreman Funeral Home moved to its present location on US Highway 84 East. Forest and Sara Hobson ran the firm until Mrs. Foreman's death in 1964 and Mr. Foreman's death in 1971. The Hobsons' eldest son, Norman, joined the firm in 1975. In 1983, the Hobsons sold their interest in the business to their son Norman and his wife, Sharon. Today, along with their son Hunter, a fourth-generation family member, the Hobsons work with their dedicated employees to serve families in the community with the same values and commitment to service that their grandparents started over 70 years ago.

Here is an early photograph of the parlor of Foreman's Funeral Home on South Three Notch Street. Probate judge J.M. Robinson purchased a casket manufacturing plant in Opp in 1924 and moved it to Andalusia, where he established the Andalusia Casket Company at the old Army Hall on North Cotton Street, now operating as Covington Casket Company under the direction of John E. and Alan Williamson. Back then, the average number of caskets produced in a week was 60.

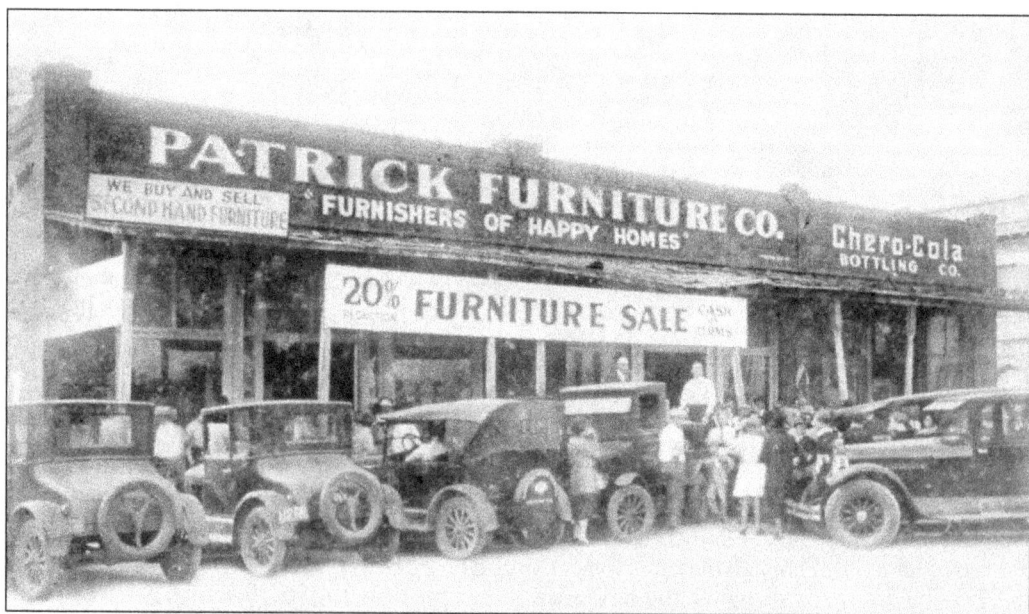

The Patrick Furniture Company advertised itself as a "Furnisher of Happy Homes," offering both cash sales and financing terms. It also bought and sold secondhand furniture. T.A. Patrick rode a bicycle to town with $100 in his pocket to start this business. The Patricks located on the west side of the square at the present site of Walker Business Machines and Home Furnishings.

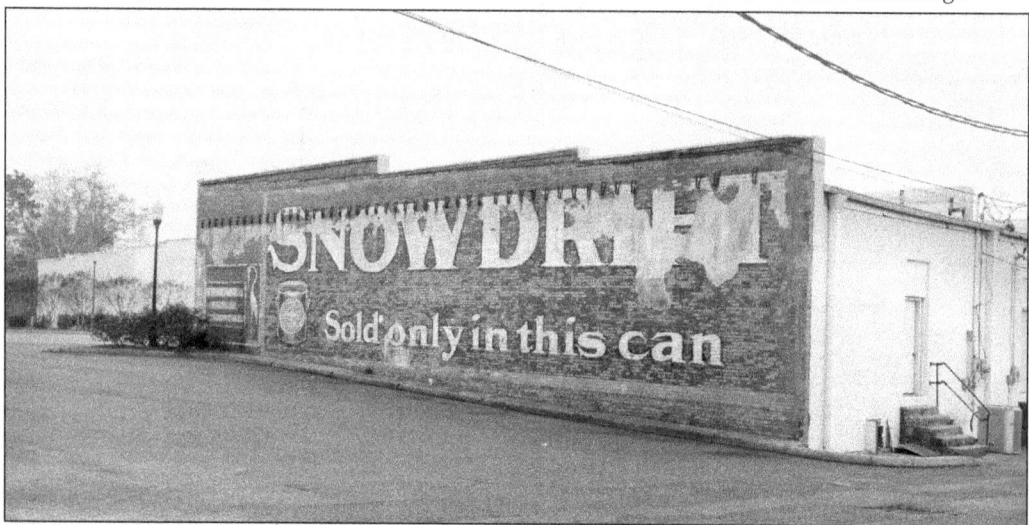

The Snead Building has this grocery advertisement featuring Snowdrift Shortening. The vintage painted sign is part of the plaza's charm, taking people back to the turn of the century and the town's earliest roots when Andalusia's commercial district had several grocery stores. Not only was cotton king throughout Alabama and the rest of the South prior to the Civil War, but it continued to be king for years afterward until the boll weevil arrived in 1915. Cotton and shortening have a connection. During the ginning process, the fluffy white fibers are separated from the seeds. As a result, the cotton gin owners were drowning in seeds and began to investigate uses for the seeds to maximize as many dollars as possible. This product is a result of that research. The Snead Building currently houses Advantage Realty, LLC; DigiPrint; the Lower Alabama Arts Coalition (LAAC); Cagle Jewelers and Goldsmithing; and Pirate Graphics. (Photograph by Robert Evers.)

Engineers reported that the lack of gates on the Gantt Dam in 1929 was to blame for the flood that year washing it and the Point "A" Dam out. Today, both dams have gates with which to control large amounts of water from the river's watershed, thus making another flood like the one in 1929 unlikely.

A 500-kilowatt steam generator was installed in 1904 in this new steam power plant at Andalusia and provided electricity to local businesses. Restored by the City of Andalusia and now known as the Power Plant Marketplace, it is used for parties and social gatherings. A farmers' market is located here and is open each year on Wednesdays and Saturdays from Memorial Day through Labor Day.

A cotton-hauling truck belonging to J.R. Caton Trucking is pictured in 1930 at the Sinclair service station on Church Street, adjacent to the Evers Building. The station was built by Dr. F.R. Smith and his son Russell in 1935. Among those pictured here are John R. Caton and sons James A. and Bethea Caton. Bethea, only 14 at the time, used to drive a truck to Pensacola, hauling his father's cotton.

WCTA Radio, with the cooperation of station owner Dige Bishop, fully supported area merchants and civic groups in the Andalusia area. In 1949, attorney Ed Reid was compared to Will Rogers for his ability to speak to schools, civic groups, and state cancer meetings as he spread the message of the seven danger signals of cancer in person and on the radio. WCTA was an AM station. "The Night Watch" by Jo Stafford was played each evening around 10:00 p.m. as the sign-off. Many Andalusians vividly remember this.

The Alonzo L. Pelham Building was constructed around 1896 on the corner of Pear and South Cotton Streets. The building once housed various drugstores, including T.M. Campbell Drug Store and then the Thagard Drug Store. Doctor offices of C.W. Wood and H.C. Battle were situated above the drugstore. Later, O.L. Thagard took in his partner Aubrey Mallette. Pharmacists Bobby Scott and Tavia Scott Tillman are still doing business as Mallette Drug Store in their location in front of Andalusia Regional Hospital.

Formerly owned by Tisdale Brooks, this drugstore on the south side of the square was sold at the close of World War II to Charles Pelham and was operated under the names Pelham Drug Company and Pelham's Walgreen. The soda fountain is remembered as a favorite teen gathering place. After school, teens flocked to the drugstore, where they jitterbugged in the back to all the old 78 records of the day.

Another downtown drugstore was the old Tom Campbell establishment at the corner of Pear and South Cotton Streets. O.L. Thagard purchased the Campbell interest and operated the store as Thagard's Drug Store until it sold to his son Lester and Aubrey Mallette. Note the sign for Dr. Battle's office upstairs. He practiced medicine as early as 1900.

This image shows the inside of the Thagard Drug Store. The store was ultimately sold to Bobby Scott, who moved the drugstore closer to Andalusia Regional Hospital, where it is today. His daughter Tavia Scott Tillman is also a pharmacist there. Pictured from left to right are Bert Windham, Clarence Boutwell, and O.L. Thagard Sr. Mallette Drug Company is still in operation today.

Opened in 1916 on River Falls Street, the Andalusia Meat Packing plant (later purchased by Swift & Company, out of Chicago) was a joint effort of businessmen and farmers recognized all over the state for efforts to diversify farming and get away from the one-crop system. The building was fireproof, had all steel-covered doors and concrete floors, and in the smoking rooms had all iron floors and iron trucks for carrying the meat. Hogs, cattle, and sheep could be efficiently handled just as in any of the largest packing plants in the country.

The Prestwood Building is featured throughout this book as one of the oldest surviving structures still in use today on the square. This image shows Dixie Studios on the second floor. Many of the photographs in the collection at the Three Notch Museum can be attributed to Dixie Studios.

This Art Deco building featured a prominent showroom window with the newest models of Chevrolets and Cadillacs on display. Count Darling Chevrolet is one of the reasons Andalusia had the reputation of having more automobiles per capita than any other town in the state. (Courtesy of David's Catfish House.)

The view in this scene looks east down Three Notch Street. The old water fountain for horses and mules is in the center. To the left is the Shreve Bros. Store, and to the right is the J.L. Knox & Co. Store. (Courtesy of David Walters.)

The old Covington Motor Company was operated by Count Darling Jr., and this was the beginning of several Chevrolet dealerships through the years in Andalusia.

In 1950, J.A. Walker operated what might be called Andalusia's first fast-food restaurant, the Dairy Queen. After three years, it was sold to Bob and Betty Bearden. They operated it until 1957, when Melvin and Euna Faulkner took over this popular main street spot frequented now for over 50 years. Their son, Jimmy Faulkner, has carried on the Dairy Queen tradition now for a number of years. (Photograph by Robert Evers.)

Dr. Juanita McDonald, a native of Tuscaloosa, was Andalusia's first practicing female physician. She was also featured on WCTA radio as part of the Parnassus Club's "Cancer Can Be Cured" Campaign. (Courtesy of Andalusia Public Library.)

Parnassus Club member Gladys Mathews Reid, the artist behind the project, poses with the locally designed scrapbook that was entered into the Federated Women's Club Service Project Contest to win $10,000. This competition took place in 1949. The wood cover was designed locally by the Southern Craftsman Furniture Company, which specialized in manufacturing fine furniture reproductions. The book is on display at the Andalusia Public library. (Courtesy of Andalusia Public Library.)

Tisdale's Sundries Company and Luncheonette was operated by Broughton Tisdale (center) and Tisdale Brooks in the Prestwood Building. This historic building also has a mural on the side depicting its rich history as a home to various drugstores and soda fountain shops.

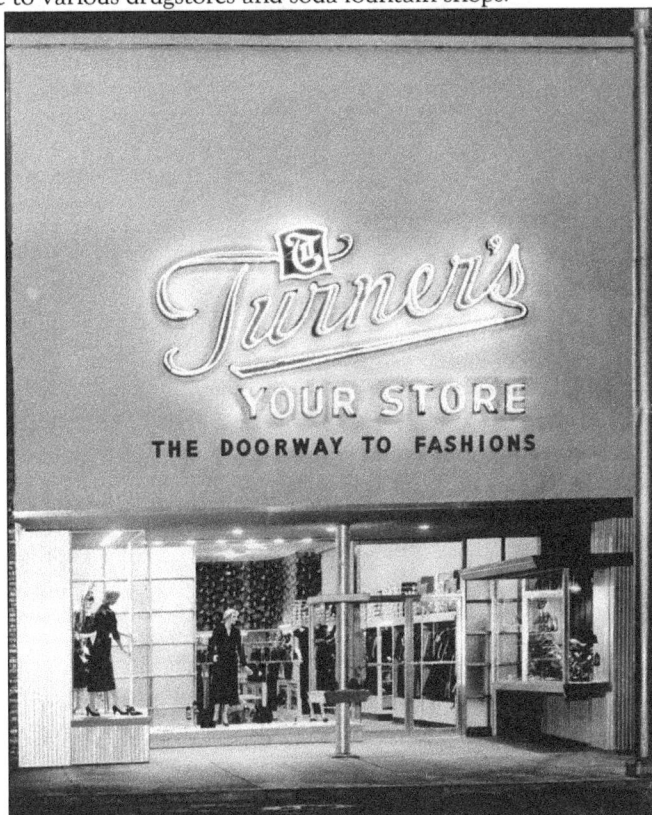

Turner's Store, owned by Sol and Rebecca Rosen, will be remembered for fine fashions and its neon sign. Its sales slogan was "Your Store: The Doorway to Fashions." Turner's was located in the Sentell Building on the court square where the law offices of Willis Wayne Bush are now.

Where the tall, six-story First National Bank Building now sits was this early saloon and pressing club. Among those pictured from left to right are A.J. Bentley; Barney McLelland; Tobe Reynolds; H.A. Lundy; Will Turner (standing in the window); G.F.C. Moore, several times commissioner; Lee Adkinson, manager of the saloon; the twin Smith brothers; Joe Aplin, chief of police at the time; Cliff Stokes with the Andalusia Coca-Cola Co.; Marcus Barron, proprietor of the Pressing Club; Ab Pelham; and Will Wyrosdick. On the second floor are Ed Dean and C.E. Harris, who came here from Georgia as an undertaker.

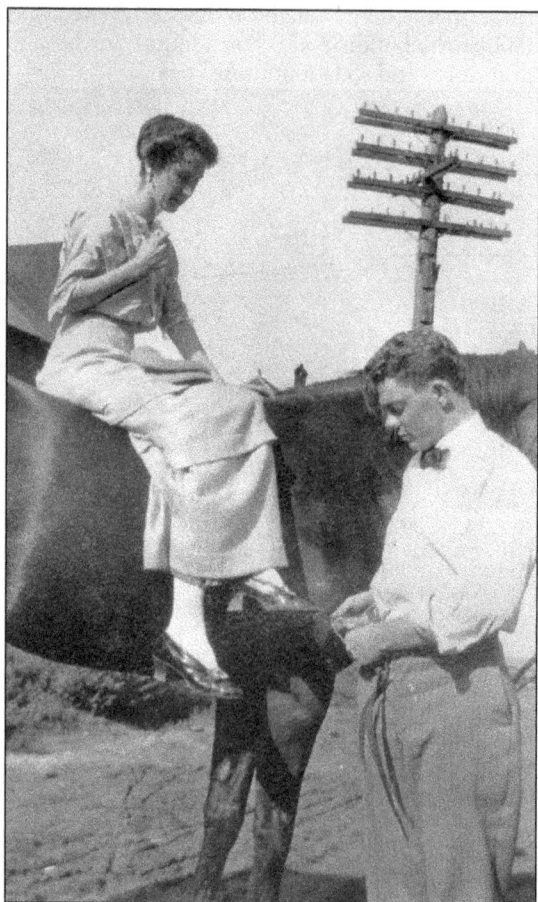

Leolive Benson's scrapbook held this 1914 image of a young couple courting. They pause on the unpaved road near a newly set power pole that brought the first transmission of electricity to homes. The young woman sits on the horse while the young man checks his timepiece. His pinstripe trousers and bow tie and her long dress and stockings were the traditional dress for an afternoon ride. (Courtesy of the Charles Gantt family.)

Eight

"ABSOLUTELY ANDALUSIA"

"Absolutely Andalusia" was the slogan used for the 2010 Celebration of Alabama Small Towns promoted by then governor Bob Riley. This new location for the Andalusia Area Chamber of Commerce is just another example of how Andalusia is prepared to partner with industry to utilize current assets in a way that can benefit industry and community. The Andalusia Area Chamber of Commerce welcomes Chrissie Shubert Duffy as the new executive director. Andalusia's elected city council includes Mayor Earl Johnson and the following council members: Will Sconiers, District 1; Ralph Wells, District 2; Kennith Mount, District 3; Hazel Griffin, District 4; Terry Powell, District 5; and John Thompson, city clerk. (Photograph by Charles W. White Jr.)

Andalusia continues to provide businesses and tourists a unique small town experience. Through the Downtown Redevelopment Authority and the Tourism and Relocation Committee, there are always projects in progress. The Gateway to Andalusia pictured here is a new asset welcoming visitors to our area. (Photograph by Robert Evers.)

The Andalusia City Hall building was constructed in 1914 and served as a school for 86 years. In 2002–2003, the building underwent a complete renovation. The project included removing walls and redesigning the space for use as a modern city hall. The building was rededicated in 2004. Today, it houses city government and hosts meetings and special events in the restored auditorium. It is the cornerstone of an era of restoration and progress in Andalusia. (Photograph by Robert Evers.)

118

The Covington County Veterans Memorial Park was dedicated on Veterans Day 2004. The park and monument were funded entirely through contributions and the sale of bricks and cornerstones. Located behind city hall, it features a 42-foot stainless steel obelisk mounted on a black granite pedestal designed and constructed by William Merrill of Wilco Welding. The pedestal is engraved with the names of soldiers who lost their lives defending the nation in various wars and conflicts. (Photograph by Robert Evers.)

The Andalusia Public Library was founded by the Study Club, established in 1913. It moved to the old post office building in 1967, after being located in a building on Sixth Avenue and College Street since 1936. In 1978, Thelma Dixon established the Charles Dixon Memorial Room, with seating for 125, a small kitchen, a stage, storage room, and restrooms. She also secured a federal matching grant to provide a piano, movie projector, and many of the chairs. Additionally, the Dixons decorated the children's room in the basement and outfitted the teen room. (Courtesy of Sue Bass Wilson.)

Church Street School was constructed from 1921 to 1923 and served as a school for 77 years. In 2010–2011, the building underwent a renovation that was a joint partnership with the Andalusia Ballet Association and the City of Andalusia. Today, Church Street Cultural Arts Centre houses the Andalusia Ballet Association and serves as an educational dance facility under the direction of Meryane Murphy. (Photograph by Robert Evers.)

The Andalusia Ballet annually performs *The Nutcracker* at the Solon and Martha Dixon Center for the Performing Arts on the campus of Lurleen B. Wallace Community College. Pictured, from left to right, are (first row) Adeline Fischer, Emily Anne Morgan, Sarah Beth Wriston, and Ada Short; (second row) Ingram Dugger, Kate Day, Emma Henley (face hidden), Rosemary Bass, and Kathleen O'Neal; (third row) Laura Syler, Abigail Lee, and Anna Duffy. (Photograph by Robert Evers.)

Andalusia High School has undergone several additions, including an auditorium, gym, band room building, and football stadium, since it was built in 1939. This year, a new wing is being added to house seventh and eighth graders on the west side of the campus. (Photograph by Robert Evers.)

In 2012, Andalusia High School dedicated its new $2.5 million indoor athletic facility. It is a 30,000-square-foot facility complete with weight room, offices, classrooms, locker rooms, and a 50-yard indoor practice field made of artificial turf. (Photograph by Charles W. White Jr.)

Andalusia Elementary School was dedicated in 2001 and is currently undergoing construction for a sixth grade wing. Rigorous academics are partnered with technology, physical education, music, and art at AES. (Photograph by Charles W. White Jr.)

The DreamPark civic project brought together 370 volunteers and all of the civic organizations in town. More than $110,000 was raised to make the entire on-campus park handicap accessible and to add 1,200 square feet of playscape, 16 new components, and new rubber surfacing. The park is adjacent to the LBW nature trail, which circles the college campus and borders the Evans Barnes Golf Course. (Courtesy of *Andalusia Star News*.)

The 1918 courthouse, shown here during the 2014 snow, still anchors the town square. Recent renovations include the relighting of the six-foot, 18-bulb chandelier that had been dark for two decades. County maintenance supervisor Kevin Kennedy has overseen the repairs for water damage, cosmetic updates, and the clock and chandelier repairs. The Covington County Courthouse includes offices for Amy Jones, circuit clerk; Janice Hart, revenue commissioner; Walt Merrill, district attorney; Ben Bowden, probate judge; Frank L. "Trippy" McGuire III, district judge (retired); Julie Sorrels Moody, district judge (appointed); and M. Ashley McKathan and Charles A. "Lex" Short, circuit court judges. (Photograph by Robert Evers.)

Andalusia has commemorated much of its history in the form of murals on many of its historic structures. The weather in Andalusia is inviting for walkers and joggers alike to enjoy murals throughout the downtown area. This mural on the side of the Clark Theatre depicts courthouse history. The murals were created by Wes Hardin. The project originated from Pat Palmore during the Mayor Jerry Andrews administration but has been continued during the administration of Mayor Earl Johnson. (Courtesy of Sue Bass Wilson.)

The Johnson Park renovations, under the leadership of parks and recreation director Dwight Mikel, included eight new ball fields, new concession stands and bathrooms, a new PA system, state-of-the-art lighting, and additional parking. The park was named in memory of J.H. Johnson, city school superintendent (1942–1964). (Photograph by Charles W. White Jr.)

William "Chick" Earl Field is the benchmark of the J.H. Johnson Park facility. A "Legends Wall" will recognize those who have supported youth sports in this county. Additionally a covered picnic pavilion was added honoring longtime city employee Duke Smith. (Photograph by Charles W. White Jr.)

PowerSouth played a huge role in bringing the Miracle League project to fruition in a relatively short period of time. The City of Andalusia spearheaded the Miracle League effort for Covington County, setting a fundraising goal of $500,000 to build the ball field and playground to accommodate children with special needs. Among those on hand was Johnny Franklin of the national Miracle League Association. He said that there are more than 275 Miracle League facilities that have been developed in the past 13 years, but he has never seen a project come together as quickly as the one in Covington County. (Photograph by Charles W. White Jr.)

"Isn't it wonderful to live in a community that takes care of the needs of all of its children?" Those were the words of PowerSouth's Gary Smith at the Miracle League field dedication. His words underscored all others spoken there. The special surface on the field and in the playground makes it easily accessible for children in wheelchairs, yet safe for anyone to play there. To date, governments, businesses, and individuals have given or pledged more than $600,000 for the project, according to Andalusia mayor Earl Johnson. (Photograph by Charles W. White Jr.)

The campus of Lurleen B. Wallace Community College would not be where it is today without the continuous support of patrons like Solon and Martha Dixon and the Dixon Foundation. The Solon and Martha Dixon Center for the Performing Arts was dedicated in 1982. The theater has seating for 500, dressing rooms for performers, a stage large enough for a symphony orchestra or ballet group, a stationary orchestra pit, and a versatile fly loft (renovated in 2010). (Photograph by Robert Evers.)

On March 15, 1968, as one of her final acts, Gov. Lurleen Burns Wallace signed the official announcement for a new junior college in Andalusia. Lurleen B. Wallace Community College, named in her honor, hosts the Lurleen Burns Wallace Memorial Room Museum. In addition to this portrait, it displays the last sweater she was knitting while receiving cancer treatments and the dress she wore to her daughter's wedding. Pictured at the unveiling of Wallace's official portrait by DiMitri Vail are, from left to right, daughter Jean Wallace (Gantt), Jack W. Wallace Sr., Betty Evans Wallace, and son Jack W. Wallace Jr. This portrait hangs in the capitol as well. (Courtesy of the Jean Wallace Gantt family.)

The Givens Home, located on 401 College Street and owned by Mr. and Mrs. Carl H. Palmer, is a perfect example of the restoration that continues in the J.W. Shreve Addition Historic District. It was built around 1915 by J.W. Barnes and became home to widow Rose Givens, her nine children, and her sister Susan Henley in 1923. An original "servant's quarters" with fireplace is still located on the property. (Photograph by Robert Evers.)

The Central of Georgia Depot, located on Historic Central Street, was completed in the spring of 1900. The depot is the oldest and only wooden commercial building remaining in downtown. Listed in the National Register of Historic Places, it was restored in 1983 by the Covington Historical Society and became the Three Notch Museum. (Courtesy of Sue Bass Wilson.)

Visit us at
arcadiapublishing.com

www.ingramcontent.com/pod-product-compliance
Lightning Source LLC
Chambersburg PA
CBHW080548110426
42813CB00006B/1251